P9-DDF-996

A LITTLE BOOK OF LANGUAGE

DAVID CRYSTAL
A LITTLE BOOK

of

LANGUAGE

YALE UNIVERSITY PRESS
NEW HAVEN AND LONDON

For information about this and other Yale University Press publications please contact:

| U.S. Office: | sales.press@yale.edu | www.yalebooks.com |
| Europe Office: | sales@yaleup.co.uk | www.yalebooks.co.uk |

Set in Minion by Yale University Press
Printed in Great Britain by TJ International Ltd, Padstow, Cornwall

Library of Congress Cataloging-in-Publication Data

Crystal, David, 1941
   A little book of language / David Crystal.
      p. cm.
   Includes bibliographical references and index.
   ISBN 978-0-300-15533-4 (alk. paper)
   1. Language acquisition. I. Title.
   P118.C74 2010
   400—dc22

                                                      2009037998

A catalogue record for this book is available from the British Library

Contents

CHAPTER 1

Baby-talk

We sometimes do some silly things with language. One of the silliest happens when we find ourselves in front of a new baby. What do we do?

We talk to it.

We probably say 'Hello' or 'What's your name?' or 'Aren't you lovely!' or something like that.

Why do we do that? The baby certainly hasn't learned any language yet. It can't possibly understand a word of what we're saying. And yet we talk to it as if it does.

The baby's mother is usually the first to strike up a conversation with it. Here's an actual example, which was audio-recorded just a few minutes after one baby was born:

Oh you are gorgeous, you are gorgeous, you are, you are, you are, oh yes you are ... hello ... hello ... aren't you beautiful ... '

And she went on like this for quite a while, while she cuddled the new arrival. The baby, meanwhile, wasn't paying the slightest attention. It had stopped crying and had its eyes shut. It may even have been asleep. But the mother didn't care. She was being totally ignored and yet she kept on talking.

And talking in a very funny way. I can't easily write down the way her voice went, but it was something like this:

Oh
  h
    h
      you
        are
          gorgeous,
           you
            are …

At the beginning of her sentence, her voice was very high, and she then let it fall all the way down. It was almost as if she was singing. When she said 'hello' her voice went very high again and she stretched the word out – 'helll–loh'. The 'aren't you beautiful' was very high too, as if she was asking a question.

The other thing she did, which we can't see from the way the words are written down, is that she rounded her lips while she spoke – puckering them as if she was giving someone a kiss. If we say something – it doesn't matter what – 'Aren't you a lovely little baby then?' – but say it with our lips pushed out as far as we can, and listen to how it sounds, it sounds like baby-talk. And that's exactly what people call it.

The lip-rounding is an important feature of baby-talk. So is the exaggerated melody of the voice. And there's another unusual feature of the way the mother was talking to her baby. She said the same thing over and over:

Oh you are gorgeous, you are gorgeous, you are, you are, you are.

Now that's not very normal. When would you ever go up to someone and say the same thing three times in a row? We don't meet a friend in the street and say:

Hi John, hi John, hi John. Coming to the shop? Coming to the shop? Coming to the shop?'

We would probably be locked up if we did that. Yet we talk like that to babies and nobody notices anything odd about it at all.

Why did the mother do it? Why do so many of us do it?

Let's think about it from mum's point of view first. She so loves that baby, and she wants to tell it so. But there's something else: she wants the baby to tell her back. Unfortunately, baby can't talk yet. But maybe, she thinks, if I can get the baby to just look at me, to see me for the first time . . . if I can just get the baby's attention . . . ?

We'll never get someone's attention if we stay quiet or say ordinary things. Instead we shout, or we whistle. We say something different, something noticeable: 'Hey, Fred! Over here! Yooo-hooo!' Think about 'Yooo-hooo!' for a moment. What a strange pair of noises to make! But we hear people make noises like that when they want someone over the road to notice them.

And we make different noises when we want to get the attention of babies. We'll never get them to notice us if we say ordinary things in an ordinary way. I've listened to many recordings of conversations with newborn babies, and nobody ever talks to them like this, in a matter-of-fact tone of voice:

Good morning. I am your mother. This is a hospital. That is a midwife. Here is a bed. Your name is Mary ...

That's the sort of language we'd use to talk to young children when they're a bit older. It's more businesslike, more informative. More like a teacher. People talk to two-year-olds like that. 'Careful. That's a hot tap. There's the cold one ...' We don't talk to new-born babies in this way.

Now think about it from the baby's point of view. Here you are, just arrived in the world, and all sorts of things are going on. It's not been all that pleasant an experience, being born, and you've been crying a lot. But things are settling down now. You're warm, and you feel comfortable, and someone is making noises at you

– nonsense noises, but still … Are they worth paying attention to? If you're hearing 'This is a hospital. That is a midwife. Here is a bed' said in an everyday, flat tone, you might well conclude that this new world is going to be deadly boring, and you might as well go back to where you came from. But if you hear 'Oh you are gorgeous' sweeping melodiously from high to low, and repeated several times, well maybe this new world is going to be interesting after all! Maybe I should open my eyes and see – ooh, some rather interesting-looking lips! So who's that, then? She looks rather nice!

Baby talk is one of the ways mothers and others develop a strong bond with their babies. And it lays the foundation for the development of language. Without realizing it, by talking to babies in this way we are beginning to teach them their mother tongue – or tongues, of course, if the baby is in a family where more than one language is spoken. By repeating the sentences, and making them noticeable, we are kick-starting the process of language learning. When people start to learn a foreign language, they know what they need in order to say their first words. They need to hear them said, over and over, loud and clear, by someone who knows how to do it. It's the same with babies. If they hear the same sounds and words and word patterns repeated, they'll soon pick the language up.

But how soon is 'soon'? How long does it take babies to learn to talk? And which bits of their mother tongue will they learn first?

BABIES, BUDGIES, AND BANGS

We talk baby-talk to babies. But there are two other occasions when we use baby-talk.

One is when we talk to animals. If we listen carefully to someone talking to a pet, what we hear is something very like what happens when we talk to babies. Indeed it can be even more peculiar. And people don't realize they're doing it. I once recorded my mum talking to her budgie, and then played it back to her afterwards. She couldn't believe she sounded so strange! But the budgie didn't think so.

And the other occasion? It's when we tease our friends, and treat them as if they're babies. Imagine: you bang your finger on something and you look to your friend for a bit of sympathy. But your friend thinks you're making a fuss about nothing. You hold up your finger. 'Look, it's sore,' you say. 'Aw did diddums hurt a lickle finger den?' asks your friend. Of course, they might not stay your friend for long, after that!

CHAPTER 2

From cries to words

It's really interesting to listen to babies during their first year of life, and try to work out what they're saying. We can learn a lot about language that way.

And the first thing we notice, if we listen to them very early on – at around one month of age, say – is that the noises they make don't sound anything like language at all. They aren't speaking. They're just vocalizing – using their voice to communicate some pretty basic needs.

We'd call it simply 'crying', a lot of the time. But the cries aren't all the same. If the baby is hungry, the hunger cry goes something like this:

```
w        w        w        w
  a        a        a        a
  a        a        a        a
    a        a        a        a
```

Each 'waa' is quite short, and there's a brief pause between each one.

If the baby is in pain, we can hear the difference straight away.

Now the cry goes something like this:

```
w
    a
     a        w
      a         a
       a         a      w
        a         a      a     w
         a         a     a     a
         a         a     a     a
```

The pain cry starts off in the high part of the voice with a huge burst of noise, then the next burst is a bit shorter and lower, and the next ones are shorter and lower still. If the baby is picked up and cuddled, the crying stops. If not, the pattern is repeated until someone comes along to comfort it.

And if the baby is content? Then the noises are quieter and more relaxed – more like gurgling. They're sometimes called 'pleasure cries'.

Now here's a question. If we couldn't see the baby, but heard only those cries, would we be able to tell which language it was learning? Do those cries sound English or French or Chinese? The answer is 'no'. At this age, babies all over the world sound the same. Researchers have done experiments to prove it. They've recorded hunger, pain, and pleasure cries from babies in different parts of the world, mixed the recordings up, and then asked listeners to sort them out. 'Can you tell which is the English baby?' they asked. No. 'Or the French one?' No. 'Or the Chinese one?' No. It can't be done.

But one year later, these same babies will definitely sound English or French or Chinese. Indeed, by then, they'll have started to say some words. So when do we begin to hear sounds from the mother-tongue in the vocal output of a child? Let's follow a baby through its first year of life, and see.

We won't notice much change in the baby cries until around three months of age. Then we'll hear something new happening.

And we can see it happening too. We'll see the baby move its lips, and vocalize at the same time, so noises come out that sound just a little like 'oo', or a bit like the 'brr' sound we make with the lips when we're cold. The gurgles at the back of the mouth also sound a little more shaped and deliberate. It's impossible to write these noises down using the letters of the alphabet, but many of them sound as if the child is saying 'goo' or 'coo' – and so this stage is usually called 'cooing'. It's a delightful stage. For the first time we get the impression that the baby is trying to tell us something.

Is there such a thing as English cooing and French cooing and Chinese cooing? No. At three months, babies with these language backgrounds still sound exactly the same.

Fast forward another three months. Now babies are trying out sounds in a much more controlled way. We'll hear sounds that we think we recognize. Some of them will be very like the sounds in the language being used around them. In particular, they can put their lips together firmly and then release them suddenly, and out pops a 'ba' or a 'pa' or a 'ma'. This feels nice, and it sounds good, so they do it several times in a row. If we say those sounds a few times – 'ba ba ba ba', 'pa pa pa pa', 'ma ma ma ma' – we'll sound like a six-month-old. People call this stage 'babbling'.

Babies babble between around six months until around nine months. They try out quite a large number of sounds during that time. We'll hear 'na na na' and 'da da da' – as well as 'bu bu bu', 'de de de', and other combinations. It's a very important stage in the development of language. It's as if they're practising. We can imagine them thinking: 'Now what happens if I push my tongue up as high as I can at the front, and bang it about a bit? That sounds good. And what if I bang my lips together a lot? Brilliant!'

And then they'd notice that some of their noises were making the adults around them very excited: 'The one with the lips, coming out as "ma-ma-ma-ma", is making that nice lady who feeds me especially pleased. And the "da-da-da-da" one seems to impress the nice man with the deep voice who bounces me up and down. And what's even more interesting is that when I do this, *they* say the noises too. It's a great game. I think I'll do it again!'

No wonder the parents get excited. In English, and in several languages, the 'ma-ma-ma' noises sound like the word for 'mummy', and the 'da-da-da' ones sound like 'daddy'. So naturally, the parents think the baby is at last saying their names. But it's not so. At this stage babies have no idea what they're saying. They're just making sounds for their own sake. If some of these sounds resemble real words, that's just a fluke. It'll be a few months more before an English-learning baby realizes that 'ma-ma' actually has a meaning.

How do we know that the baby has no idea what it's saying? Because we hear the same 'ma-ma-ma' sound being used in all sorts of situations, whether the mother is there or not. Imagine learning a word in a foreign language, such as French – the word 'porte', for instance. It means 'door'. But if we were heard saying 'porte' when we saw a cat, or an apple, or a bed, people would quickly conclude that we had no idea what 'porte' meant. They'd change their minds only when they heard us saying it every time we saw a door. It's the same with babies. There will come a time when they will learn that, in English, 'mama' is the sound they need to use when they want to talk about 'mother', or call for her. At six months of age, they haven't reached that stage.

Fast forward another three months. Now something really important happens. One thing I didn't mention, when I talked about babbling, is that the sounds come out in a rather random, jerky way. We might hear a 'ba-ba-ba-ba', but only the first 'ba' is strongly pronounced. The others are made less firmly, and not very consistently, and the sequence as a whole doesn't have any definite shape. But at around nine months, for the first time, we'll hear sequences like 'ba-ba' which *do* have a shape. They are beginning to sound like real words. How do babies manage to do this?

It's because they have begun to learn two of the most important features of language. One is rhythm; the other is intonation. I'll talk about intonation in a moment. Rhythm is the 'beat' a language has. In a language like English, we can hear that beat if we say a sentence out loud, and clap each time we hear a strong sound. In this sentence:

I think it's time we went to town.

the strong beats are on 'think', 'time', 'went', and 'town'. And the rhythm of the sentence as a whole is 'te-tum-te-tum-te-tum-te-tum'.

Now this sort of rhythm is typical of English. We can hear it in a lot of poetry, for instance. It's widely used in nursery rhymes like this one:

The grand old Duke of York
He had ten thousand men.

This is 'te-tum-te-tum-te-tum' twice over. And it's the favourite poetry pattern of William Shakespeare. If we go to see one of his plays, this is the main kind of rhythm we'll hear the characters use.

But it's not a rhythm that we'll hear in every language. French people don't speak their language like that. Their speech has a rhythm which is more like 'rat-a-tat-a-tat-a-tat'. And Chinese people don't speak their language like that either. When English people hear Chinese people talking, they often describe the speech as 'sing-song'.

At around nine months of age, then, babies start to give their utterances a bit of a beat, reflecting the rhythm of the language they're learning. The utterances of English babies start to sound like 'te-tum-te-tum'. The utterances of French babies start to sound like 'rat-a-tat-a-tat'. And the utterances of Chinese babies start to sound like sing-song. Of course, none of their utterances are very lengthy yet. These babies aren't telling their mum 'I think it's time we went to town' or reciting 'The Grand Old Duke of York'. But they *are* trying out tiny utterances, such as 'mama' and 'dada', and these sound like real words. The utterances don't have a clear meaning yet, but they are being pronounced more confidently and consistently. We get the feeling that real language is just around the corner.

This feeling is reinforced by the other feature of language I mentioned a little while ago: intonation. Intonation is the melody or music of a language. It refers to the way the voice rises and falls as we speak. How might we tell someone that it's raining?

It's raining, isn't it! (or 'innit', perhaps)

We're *telling* the person, so we give our speech a 'telling' melody. The pitch-level of our voice falls and we sound as if we know what we're talking about. We're making a statement. But now imagine we *don't* know if it's raining or not. We think it might be, so we're asking someone to check. We can use the same words – but note the question-mark, this time:

It's raining, isn't it?

Now we're *asking* the person, so we give our speech an 'asking' melody. The pitch-level of our voice rises and we sound as if we're asking a question.

So now I can answer the question I asked at the end of Chapter 1. Which bits of their mother tongue do babies learn first? Answer: the rhythm and the intonation. If we mixed up audio-recordings of nine-month-old English, French, and Chinese babies, and asked people to identify where they came from, they could do it. The English-learning babies are beginning to sound English. The French ones are beginning to sound French. And the Chinese ones are beginning to sound Chinese. We can hear a rhythm and an intonation that sound familiar.

By the time babies reach their first birthday, they've usually begun to develop their intonation patterns, using them to express different notions. There's an old song which goes 'It ain't what you say but the way that you say it'. That's something that stays with us all our life. We often hear someone say something and think 'It wasn't what he said, it was the way he said it that annoyed me'. As we'll see in a later chapter, tone of voice is a very important way of conveying meaning. And babies start using tones of voice to do this at around one year of age.

I have a recording of one of my children at around this age. He heard footsteps on the path outside and he said 'dada' with a high questioning intonation: it meant 'is that daddy?' Then I walked into the room, and he said 'dada', with a strong falling intonation – it meant 'Yes it *is* daddy'. Then he put out his arms and said 'dada' with an appealing intonation – it meant 'Pick me up, daddy'. Later, when he'd learned how to string words together, he would be able to say properly: 'Is that daddy?', 'Yes it is daddy', 'Pick me up, daddy!' A question, a statement, and a command. But he couldn't string words together at 12 months, because he only had one: 'dada'.

When did he learn 'dada'? When do children learn their magical 'first word'? And when do they start stringing words together to make sentences? That's the next stage in the amazing process of language acquisition.

LISTENING BEFORE WE'RE BORN

Babies can hear things in their mother's womb before they're born. It normally takes nine months for a baby to grow from being just a group of tiny cells to being ready to come out into the world. And after it's been in the womb for about six months, its little ears, and all the pathways inside its head that allow it to hear, are fully formed. So it can hear any noises going on around it.

How do we know what a baby can hear? Sometimes it's necessary for doctors to insert a probe into the womb, to check on how the baby is developing. It's very easy to insert a tiny microphone at the same time, and listen in. That way we can hear what the baby can hear.

And what does the baby hear? The mother's heart beat. Blood sloshing through the veins of the body. Tummy-rumbles. And – the mother's voice. When she speaks, the baby can hear the voice in the distance – a bit like how we hear when we put our fingers in our ears. If we do that and get someone to talk to us, the voice sounds very muffled and distant. We might not be able to pick out all the words, but we can certainly hear the rhythm and intonation. Babies are getting practice in listening to those features of language before they're even born. That is probably why they are the first features of language they learn.

When the baby is born, we can do another interesting experiment. Researchers put headphones on the tiny ears and play some sounds – a dog barking, a man's voice, a woman's voice, the mother's voice. They put a teat into the baby's mouth and wire it up to a counter. The baby sucks away at a steady rate. When it hears the dog, man, and woman sounds, the sucking speeds up a bit and then slows down. But when it hears the mother's voice it sucks like crazy! It recognizes her.

We can do this experiment when the baby is just a few hours old. Babies don't have to wait to learn what mummy sounds like. They know already.

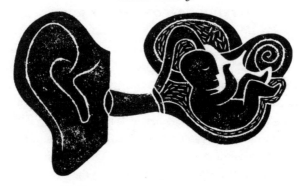

CHAPTER 3

Learning how to understand

Let's think about what happens when we learn a word. If I say that in Japanese there's a word *bara-bara*, and ask you to learn it, what's the first question you'll ask me?

'What does it mean?'

That's a very sensible question, because there isn't much point in trying to learn a word if you don't know what it means. (Actually it means 'very heavy rain', and it's an extremely useful word to know if you're thinking of walking around Tokyo without an umbrella!)

But what if you're a baby, and you can't ask 'What does it mean?' because you haven't learned to talk yet? Now what do you do?

You watch and you listen. You pay attention to what's going on around you. There's plenty to listen to, after all. People are talking to you all the time, except when you're having a meal or about to fall asleep. And there's plenty of time to listen, because actually you haven't got much else to do. While you're awake and not eating, all you can do is lie back and take in your new world – how it looks, how it feels, how it smells, how it sounds. And especially, how it sounds when the noises come out of another human being.

There's something special about the sound of speech. We heard it before we were born. And after we were born we heard it being used in wonderfully melodic ways. It will never cease to amaze us. Eventually we come to realize that language is the most wonderful tool for expressing our thoughts and feelings, and that it is language, more than anything else, which makes us feel human. Animals can communicate with each other, as we'll see later, but they don't have anything to match human language.

Babies love to listen. We can tell, because when they hear a sound their head turns towards it. That's the main way hearing specialists – they're called audiologists – can tell whether a young baby's ears are working properly. The audiologist stands behind the child and makes a noise, such as ringing a small bell. If the baby hears it, its head will turn in the direction of the sound. If its head doesn't move after several tries, then doctors will carry out investigations to see if the child is deaf.

Babies also *want* to listen. They *want* to learn language. Now when I say 'want' I don't mean that they're deliberately thinking about it, in the way that you or I might 'want' a bike or a new computer. What I mean is that a baby's brain is set up in such a way that it is *ready* for languages. It is looking out for them, waiting to be stimulated and activated by them. Language researchers sometimes talk about the baby brain containing a 'language acquisition device'. They think of it as a huge network of cells which has evolved over thousands of years to help humans learn to talk to each other as early in their lives as possible. We shouldn't be surprised that babies learn languages – and learn them so quickly. It's what they're designed to do.

Note that I said 'languages', not 'a language'. Three-quarters of the babies in the world learn more than one language. Some learn four or five at the same time. That amazes people who are used to living in a community where only one language is spoken, but it's all perfectly normal. We have to think of it from the babies' point of view. All they know is that people are talking to them. They have no idea that the words belong to different languages. They won't realize that until they're older. If mummy speaks one way and daddy speaks another and the lady in the shop speaks in a third way, so what? They're only words, after all. Babies pick it all up naturally, like breathing.

The human brain can cope with dozens of languages. And

I mean dozens. One man, a journalist called Harold Williams, showed just what can be done. He was the foreign editor of *The Times* newspaper in the early 1900s. He went to an international meeting in 1918, called the League of Nations, and was able to talk to each of the delegates in their own language. He could speak 58 languages fluently! That deserves several exclamation marks: 58!!! It makes learning just two languages – being bilingual – seem quite a small task, really.

So, out of all the bits and pieces which make up a language, a baby first homes in on rhythm and intonation, as we saw in Chapter 2. But what comes next? Parents know the answer to that question, for they're eagerly looking out for it as their baby comes towards the end of its first year of life. And when it happens, they're delighted. What is it?

A word.

A first word.

Babies quickly notice words, in the speech around them. This is because, when we speak, some words, and some parts of words, sound much louder than others. They stand out. Imagine this situation. We're playing with a baby, and a dog comes into the room. What are we likely to say to the baby? Something like this, probably:

Oh look! It's a dog. Hello, doggie …

Now, how would we say all that? Which bits would we emphasize? Say the sentences out loud, and listen to which parts come out most strongly. It goes like this:

Oh <u>look</u>! It's a <u>dog</u>. Hel<u>lo</u>, <u>dog</u>gie.

And those are the parts that the baby notices. From the baby's point of view, our sentences would sound something like this:

look … dog … lo … dog

Notice how some words get repeated. Without realizing it, we are teaching the baby the word 'dog'.

Do babies understand what we're saying? It's often difficult to tell. But sometimes we can see, from the way they react, that they do know what a word is referring to. I once did a little experiment to show this, using my son Steven when he was about a year old. I sat him on the floor surrounded by some toys, including a toy bus, a ball, and a teddy bear. He wasn't paying them any special attention. But when I asked him, 'Where's your ball?' he looked at it straight away and stretched out his hands for it. Then after he'd played with it for a while, I said, 'Where's your teddy?' and he looked around for that. After another little while I said 'Where's your bus?' This time he didn't make any movement.

Steven seemed to know the words 'ball' and 'teddy', but not 'bus'. Of course he might have known 'bus' too, and just didn't bother looking for that toy. Maybe he was getting bored with the game. Or maybe he was thinking: 'I'm fed up being the subject of an experiment. I want my dinner!' But he gave definite signs that he understood the other two words.

People who study children's language spend a lot of time watching how babies react to the speech they hear around them. They make films of adults and babies interacting, and examine them very carefully to see whether the babies show any signs of understanding what the adults say. Sometimes the signs are very subtle – slight movements of the baby's eyes or the head or the hands. You'd never notice them if you were just sitting with the child, but by watching a recording over and over you can spot them.

How many words did Steven know by the time he was 12 months? I felt he knew about a dozen. He certainly knew 'mummy' and 'daddy', as well as 'ball', 'teddy', 'drink', and a few other names of things. He could also link some words with the activities they related to. For instance, after playing a tickling game, such as 'round and round the garden', we would say 'again?', in a questioning tone of voice – and his excited body language left us in no doubt that he wanted to play it another time. 'Peep-bo' was another playtime expression he recognized. He knew that if he knocked over a pile of bricks, someone was likely to say 'down'. And he knew that after all the food in a bowl was finished he would hear 'all gone'. Some of these words he seemed to recognize very early on, from around six months of age.

The words in a language are called its *vocabulary*. Steven was beginning to learn the vocabulary of English. Notice that he was doing this in two stages. The first stage was to understand some of the words he heard being used around him. But at 12 months he hadn't yet learned how to say any of them for himself. When people actively use words themselves we say they have an *active vocabulary*. When they understand words but don't actually use them, we say they have a *passive vocabulary*. At 12 months, Steven had a passive vocabulary of a dozen words, and an active vocabulary of none.

But that was about to change. A week or so after that little experiment, he produced his first word. His doting parents were delighted. They'd been waiting breathlessly. Was it going to be 'mummy' or 'daddy'?

It was neither. It was 'all gone'.

You can never predict what a child's first word is going to be. Many children's first words are indeed those for 'mummy' or 'daddy' in their language. But often it's an unexpected first word, expressing something the child has found especially important. One child's first word was 'car'. Another child said 'bic' (meaning 'biscuit') first. Another said 'cat'. Another said 'more'. And Steven said 'all gone'.

That looks like two words, doesn't it? 'All' + 'gone'. But Steven didn't know that yet. All he heard was a series of sounds with two rhythmical beats in it. And that's how he said it: it came out more or less like 'awdaw', as if it was a single word. He couldn't pronounce the sounds properly yet, of course. He couldn't make a 'g' sound, so the word 'gone' came out beginning with 'd'. And he didn't seem to have heard the sounds at the end of 'all' and 'gone'. (We'll see why they were a problem in a later chapter.) But he did the rest.

Once Steven got his tongue round one word, it wasn't long before his active vocabulary began to grow. He tried another and another. Within a month he was speaking about 10 words. By 18 months his active vocabulary had grown to about 50 words. And his passive vocabulary had also grown. He was able to understand at least 200 words. He was well on his way to language.

HOW MANY WORDS DO YOU KNOW?

Every language in the world has thousands and thousands of words, and one of the jobs that language researchers do is collect them into books, called *dictionaries*, where we can look them up if we're not sure what they mean.

How many do you know? I bet you have no idea. I've asked a lot of people this question. One said 500. Another said 1,000. Another said 5,000. They're all miles out.

Have you understood all the words in this book so far? If you have, then you've coped with over 800 different words. And that's just in 20 pages. By the time you've finished this book the total will be several thousand. You'll learn a few new words, of course, to do with the study of language, but most of the words in this book you knew before you started to read it.

And they are only a small proportion of the words that are in your head. This book is only about language, so its vocabulary is going to be quite restricted. It's not about space exploration or sports cars or clothes or food or television programmes, or all the hundreds of other things that we deal with day by day. Just think how many words there must be to talk about clothes, for instance. Or all the words for animals that you know. Or all the weird words there are in the *Harry Potter* or *Lord of the Rings* books.

Most people entering their teens have a vocabulary of at least 20,000 words, and this grows really fast as they go up through the school and learn about more specialized topics in history, geography, physics, and so on. Most adults have a vocabulary about twice that. And if you've gone to university, learned a subject in real depth, and kept up with your reading, your vocabulary will be at least twice as much again.

If you've got the time, you can check all this out for yourself. A dictionary of about 1,500 pages gives us information about 100,000 different words. You can read through it, word by word, and count up the ones you know. It'll only take you a month!

CHAPTER 4

Making vibrations

My son Steven understood 'all gone' when he was about six months old. But he didn't try to say it until he was one year old. Even then he didn't say it properly. Why was there such a delay? And why couldn't he say it right first time?

If you've started to learn a foreign language, you'll know the answer. Some of the sounds of a new language are different, and it takes a while to work out how to pronounce them. Where do we put our tongue? How do we shape our lips? Some people are brilliant, and have the ability to copy strange sounds accurately without any problem at all. Most of us aren't so lucky: we have to practise, practise, practise.

That's what babies have to do. They're starting from scratch, remember. They have to work out where everything goes – tongue, lips, the lot. It's a complicated business, and it takes several months to sort it all out.

What is 'the lot'? Which parts of our body do we use when we talk? They're called the *vocal organs*, and there are more of them than we might think. Some, like our lips, we can easily see. Others are hidden, but we can feel them. Some are very tiny. And others are really quite large.

The largest are our lungs. Now, you might not have thought that the lungs are 'vocal' organs. After all, they're in our chest, a long way from our mouth. But without our lungs, we wouldn't be able to talk at all. Speech needs a stream of air to carry the sounds. And that airstream begins in our lungs.

Let's just think for a moment about how we hear sounds. If I am on one side of the street and you are on the other, how is it that I can hear you if you call out to me? We can't see anything linking the two of us. How does the sound get across the road?

It's carried along by the air. The movements you make with your vocal organs cause vibrations in the air, and these travel across the road as a series of invisible movements called *sound waves*. The sound waves then enter my ears and activate a network of tiny bones and cells which enable me to hear you. A special nerve called the *auditory nerve* then sends the waves on to my brain where I recognize the sounds and work out what you've said.

None of this could happen if there weren't some air to carry the sounds to the ears in the first place. And we get this air from our lungs. When we breathe in, our lungs pull in quite a lot of air. When we breathe out, we use this air to carry our speech sounds.

What's interesting is the way we change our normal pattern of breathing to enable us to speak. Normally we breathe in and out every two or three seconds. You can time it, if you like. Look at a watch and see how many times you breathe in and out in a minute. If you're resting, it'll be about 25 times. If you've just been running it'll be twice as many.

When we speak, something happens to our breathing. We breathe in quickly and then we let out the air very, very slowly. It might be five or ten seconds before we breathe in again. Some people can speak for quite a long time before needing to breathe in. How much can *you* say in one breath? Breathe in and start counting slowly: 'one, two, three …' You should be able to get up to nine or ten easily. If you take a really deep breath, you might get up to 20.

So when we speak, we have to do three things. First we have to decide what we want to say. That activity takes place in our brain. Then our brain has to send a message to our lungs to slow down the flow of air. And then we have to actually shape the sounds that will make up our speech. How do we do that? If we follow the air as it moves from our lungs to our mouth, we'll see.

The air first moves from our lungs through our windpipe into our throat, and on the way it passes between the *vocal folds*. They're sometimes called *vocal cords*, but 'cords' always makes me think of something like pieces of string, and they're not at all like that. *Folds* is a better word, because they are actually two flaps of tissue stretching across our windpipe, joined at one end. Doctors can look down our windpipe using a special mirror. This is what they see:

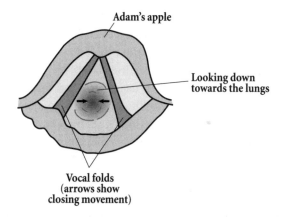

Adam's apple

Looking down towards the lungs

Vocal folds
(arrows show
closing movement)

Where are the vocal folds, exactly? If you gently feel the front of your neck, you'll notice a hard part that sticks out. It's called the *Adam's apple*. The Adam's apple is there to protect the vocal folds, which lie just behind it. The part where the two folds join is at the front. You can get a sense of where they are by coughing. Try it. Cough gently, and feel where in your neck the cough comes from. What actually happens when you cough is that the muscles in your throat make the two vocal folds come tightly together. You let the air build up underneath them. And then you release the air in a sudden noisy burst.

Or hold your breath. Try it. What's happening now? You've brought the vocal folds tightly together again, and stopped your breath from coming out. You can feel the muscles in your neck and chest holding the breath in. When you want to let the breath out, you just relax the muscles. The vocal folds separate, making a tiny audible gasp, and you start breathing normally again.

It's just as well that we have vocal folds which close like this. Holding our breath helps us build up pressure so that we can lift or push things. And shutting the vocal folds helps to stop food and liquids entering our lungs. We've all had the experience of things 'going down the wrong way' when we've eaten or drunk something carelessly. What's happened is that we haven't swallowed properly. When we swallow, we close off our windpipe. If we eat or drink in a rush, we don't time our swallowing right, the windpipe stays open, and we end up coughing and spluttering. It's not a very nice experience, and it can even be dangerous. Some people have ended up in hospital after choking on their food.

It's amazing to see how, over thousands of years of evolution, human beings have learned to use their vocal folds to help them speak. We've done it by controlling the way we make them vibrate. A vibration occurs when something goes backwards and forwards so fast that we can hardly see the movement, but we can feel it – such as when a mobile phone vibrates in our pocket, or when a washing machine is spinning around. We can easily create a vibration by stretching an elastic band between our fingers and flicking it. The movement is a blur, but we feel the vibration as a tickly sensation on our fingers.

We can make our vocal folds vibrate like that, when we speak, as air passes between them. We don't realize it, but they're vibrating a hundred times or more every second. And we can make them vibrate faster or slower. If we make them vibrate very slowly, we make a sound low down in our voice. We say it has a low *pitch*. If we make them vibrate very quickly, we make a sound high up. It has a high pitch. The same thing happens when we sing. If we sing low notes, our vocal folds are vibrating slowly. If we sing higher ones, they vibrate faster. If we sing a very high note, we can feel the tension in our neck as we keep the vocal folds vibrating at high speed.

How fast do the folds vibrate? Men, women, and children are all different. Men speak lower than women, and men and women speak lower than children. There's lots of variation, of course.

Some men have a very deep voice, and some have quite a high-pitched voice. Some women have a shrill voice and some have a low-pitched voice. It's never easy to predict the type of voice people will have just by looking at them. Will a very large man have a very deep voice? Not always.

Most men, when they're talking, make their vocal folds vibrate at around 120 times a second. When the intonation of their speech falls, the speed reduces to maybe around 90 vibrations a second; and when it rises, the vibrations might go as high as 350 a second. Some men with bass voices can go down very low indeed, with the vocal folds vibrating extremely slowly, around 50 or 40 times a second. You can see a man called Tim Storms on YouTube make his voice go down so low – to around 8 vibrations a second – that you can't even hear it any more. But the vibrations are still there. He puts his mouth by a cup of water, and you can see the vibrations from his vocal folds making the surface of the water move.

Most women have higher voices than men. When they're talking, they make their vocal folds vibrate around 200 times a second. When their intonation falls, their vibrations go down to around 150 a second; and when it rises they can go up to around 1,000. The pitch of soprano singers can go much higher than that, reaching 1,500 or more vibrations a second.

Most children have quite a high voice. When they're talking, their vocal folds are vibrating around 300 times a second. Their voices don't get much lower, but they can certainly get a lot higher, as everyone knows who has heard a group of fans screaming at a pop concert. The vocal folds go into overdrive then!

Sometime during the teenage years, the voice 'breaks', due to the hormone changes that are taking place in the body. Both boys and girls find their voices getting lower, and with boys the changes are really noticeable. Boy sopranos and altos become tenors and basses. It's actually a bit misleading to use the word 'break', as the change usually doesn't happen overnight. It might take several weeks for a boy's voice to deepen.

It's possible to feel the vibrations of the vocal folds. Make the sound 'ah', and hold it for a few seconds, as if you're singing. Now gently put your thumb and finger on either side of your Adam's apple. Don't press too hard. You should be able to feel the vibration through the skin. If you find it difficult, try it on a friend. It's often easier to feel the vibration in someone else's throat.

But here's something only you can do. *Hear* the vibration. To do this, practise saying 'sssss' and 'zzzzz' one after the other. Now put your fingers in your ears and say them again. With 'sssss' you'll not hear much. But with 'zzzzz' you'll be surprised at how loud the sound is. That's the effect of the vibration coming up into your head.

When sounds are vibrating in this way, like 'zzzzz', we call them *voiced* sounds. When sounds are made without the vocal folds vibrating, like 'sssss', we call them *voiceless* sounds. When we whisper, there's no vibration at all. The voice is very quiet. When we talk normally, the loudness comes from the way we make some of the sounds with very strong vibrations.

For Steven to say 'all gone', he had to learn all of this. He had to make his vocal folds vibrate all the way through. And he had to make them switch from quite fast to quite slow, because the 'all' was said at a higher pitch than the 'gone'. It was almost sing-song. That's how adults usually say 'all gone' to their babies, of course. And Steven picked it up perfectly. Out it came, like this:

Aw

    daw

Excellent vocal-fold control, Steven! But, hold on a moment: where are the 'l', the 'g', and the 'n'? And the 'a' in 'all' should sound different from the 'o' in 'gone'. Why aren't you doing that?

'Give us a chance,' he might have said (if he could have talked). 'I'm only twelve months.' And indeed, a few months later, he was able to say 'all gone' like you and me. What more did he have to learn in order to do that?

HOW THE ADAM'S APPLE GOT ITS NAME

The story goes that, in the Garden of Eden, Eve gave Adam an apple to eat. He wasn't used to apples, of course, and a piece stuck in his throat. Eve didn't have the same problem. That's why men's Adam's apples stick out more than women's do.

The real reason is far less exciting. It was probably due to a bad translation from the Hebrew language, in which the Bible was written. In Hebrew, the word for 'man' is 'adam' and the word for 'bump' is very similar to the word for 'apple'. So when people translated the phrase into other languages, instead of working out that it meant 'bump of man' they thought it meant 'apple of Adam'. And the name stayed.

CHAPTER 5

Pronouncing sounds

What happens to the air, after it passes through our vocal folds and moves on up our throat? Eventually, it leaves our bodies, going out either through our mouth or through our nose. When we're just breathing normally, it goes out through our nose. When we speak, most of it goes out through our mouth. And that's where things start to happen.

When the air flows through the mouth, it's a bit like wind going through a tunnel. The difference is that we can change the shape of the tunnel by moving our tongue and our lips, and also our jaw. Each time we make a new shape, we make a new sound. It only takes a tiny movement to change one sound into another. Human beings can make hundreds of sounds with their mouths, though only some of these are used in a single language.

If a baby is learning the English language, it has to master over 40 different sounds, sooner or later. It also has to string them together in all kinds of different ways, to make up words. Because we've been doing it for years, we forget how tricky it was when we were learning. We can make the tongue dance all over the mouth now, without a second thought. We can actually feel the dancing in some words. If we say the opening line of the nursery rhyme 'Hickory dickory dock', we can feel the tongue flicking along the roof of the mouth.

Let's take one of those words and see just what is involved in pronouncing it correctly: 'dock'. It's got four letters in it, but there are actually only three sounds:

a [d] sound at the beginning
an [o] sound in the middle
and a [k] sound at the end, spelled with two letters 'ck'.

Why is [k] spelled with two letters instead of one? I'll talk about that in a later chapter.

Have you noticed that I've suddenly started to put the names of the sounds into square brackets? That's what people who study speech do. It's to make it clear that they're talking about sounds rather than spellings. From now on, every time you see a letter in square brackets, I'm talking about a sound.

So, how do we pronounce a [d] sound? Make it several times: [da-da-da-da]. We press the tongue up hard against the ridge behind our teeth, and hold it there for a fraction of a second. The air coming up from our lungs suddenly finds it can't get out, so it builds up behind the blockage. Then we suddenly drop our tongue, and out pops all the air in a rush. It's like a mini-explosion.

We make a [t] sound in exactly the same way. Try [ta-ta-ta-ta]. Once again, the tongue presses up hard against the teeth ridge, and we hold it there. Once again, the air can't get out. And once again, when we drop the tongue, there's a mini-explosion.

So what's the difference between a [d] and a [t]? If the mouth is making the same shape for both sounds, how come we hear them as different? This is where the vocal folds come into play. When we make a [d] sound, the vocal folds are vibrating: it's a voiced sound. When we make a [t] sound, they're not: it's a voiceless sound. The same sort of buzz that we heard when we went [zzzzz] is actually there when we say [d] – only we can't hear it so much, because the [d] sound is said very quickly, whereas a [z] sound lasts longer.

Now it's possible to see why a baby has such a job learning to pronounce sounds. To get [d] right, the baby has to put its tongue in the right place, hold it there for the right amount of time, and then pull the tongue away quickly and in the right direction to make the next sound – and also, at exactly the right moment, make its vocal folds vibrate. It takes quite a lot of practice to get everything working together properly. But the baby has been getting a lot of practice, of course. As we saw in Chapter 2, it said [d] thousands of times when it was babbling. No wonder my son Steven managed it perfectly.

Every sound in the language is like this. The tongue has to be in the right place at the right time. We have to start and stop the vocal folds vibrating. Sometimes we have to get our lips into the right place too – as when we pronounce such sounds as [b] or [p]. And sometimes we have to shape our tongue in a special way, to get the sound right – as when we pronounce a [s] or a [l]. It takes children several years to get all the sounds right. Most of them are being pronounced well by the time a child is three, but some of the more difficult sounds take a lot longer to master.

The task isn't just one of learning a single sound. Children have to learn to string the sounds together, and that can be tricky too. They might be able to say 'sing' but have difficulty putting two sounds together at the front of a word in order to say 'sting'. And then, when they've mastered that, they still find it difficult to say one word with three sounds together, as in 'string'. Even at age six or seven, we can hear some children saying 'stwing'. Making a [r] sound after a [t] is really quite hard.

Poor old Steven had already had a lesson in hard sounds. He had tried to say 'all gone' and out had come 'aw-daw'. He couldn't manage the [g]. To make a [g] sound, you have to press the back part of your tongue hard against the roof of the mouth: [ga-ga-ga-ga]. Most children at his age find this a lot harder to do than to make a [d] sound at the front of the mouth.

He must have been able to hear that [g] was one of those sounds where there's a buzzing and a mini-explosion at the same time, so he gave it his best shot. But he put the front of his tongue up instead of the back, and out came [d]. Better luck next time, Steven!

And why couldn't he make the [n] sound in 'gone'? That's because, to pronounce a [n] he had to do something even trickier.

He had to let the air come out of his nose – [n] is a *nasal* sound. There are only three nasal sounds in English: [n], [m] as in 'mum', and [ng] as at the end of 'sing'. In each case, to make the sound, the air doesn't flow out of the mouth, but goes up into the nose and out that way.

How do we do that? If we open our mouth wide and look in a mirror at the very back of our throat, we'll see a downwards-hanging rounded piece of flesh, attached to the back part of the roof of the mouth. It's called the *uvula* – pronounced '*you*-view-la'. We can see it more clearly when we say 'ah', because doing that lowers our tongue a little. That's why, when we have a sore throat and go to the doctor, we're told to 'say ah'. It's easier for the doctor to see the back of the throat that way.

We can't see or feel it happening, but we can move that part of our mouth up and down. When we breathe normally, we keep it down, so that the air goes straight up into our nose and out. When we move it up, we press it against the back part of our throat, so that the air can't get out that way any longer, and has to come out of the mouth.

It's amazing how much work the back part of the mouth does. If we say a sentence like 'My Auntie Mary went running into town to get some bananas', it goes up and down no less than eleven times, to make all the sounds. Can you identify all the nasal sounds? I've underlined them here:

M̲y Au̲ntie M̲ary we̲nt ru̲nni̲ng i̲nto tow̲n to get so̲me ba̲na̲nas.

The air goes out of the nose for the 'M', then out of the mouth for the 'y' and the 'Au', then out of the nose for the 'n', then out of the mouth for the 'tie', and so on. For a word like 'bananas' the back of the mouth goes up and down like a – I was going to say 'yo-yo', but it's very much faster than that.

Steven certainly knew how to do this. He could say 'mama' very well – that's down-and-up twice in quick succession. But he didn't do it at the end of the word 'gone'. Why not? Maybe his problem was that he couldn't hear the [n] sound clearly. It's a fairly quiet sound, after all. Not a big noisy brute like [d] or [s].

That's probably what happened. When we look at Steven's 'aw-daw', we can see that he had a go at saying the loudest sounds of the words 'all gone'. He missed out the sounds at the end of each word – the [l] and the [n] – and they are the quietest sounds in that phrase. Most young children do this: they pronounce sounds at the beginning and in the middle of words before they say the sounds at the ends.

Still, it was a brave effort. Steven has started down the English-speaking road. Within a few months he had picked up several more sounds, and by the age of three he had got his tongue round almost all of them. Meanwhile, his cousin who lives in Paris was doing the same thing – but with French sounds. And his friend from next door was doing the same thing – but with Welsh and English sounds at the same time! He would be bilingual one day.

But what is the point of learning sounds? Sounds by themselves have no meaning. It doesn't make sense to ask 'What does [t] mean?' or 'What does [s] mean?' – [t] or [s] don't have any meaning. But when we combine sounds to make up words, and go on to join these words together to make up sentences, *then* we start to mean something. Let's see how that happens.

THE VOCAL ORGANS

Here's a drawing which shows how all the vocal organs fit together. We can make hundreds of different sounds by moving our lips, teeth, tongue, and uvula in different ways, and by changing the vibration of the vocal folds. When we speak English, we use only a few of these sounds; but we can study them all, if we take up a subject called *phonetics*. A *phonetician* is someone who studies all the possible speech sounds a human being can make.

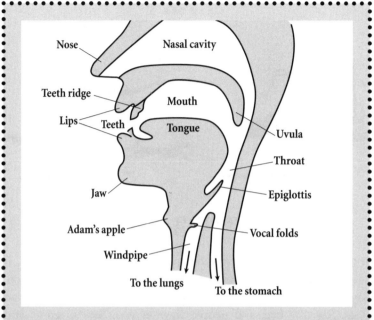

These sounds are usually divided into two types: *consonants* and *vowels*. Consonants are the sounds we make when our tongue or lips briefly block the sound from coming out of the mouth, either completely, as for [b] or [m], or almost completely, as for the 'hissy' sounds like [f] and [z]. Vowels are sounds like [a], [e], and [u], which we make when our mouth doesn't block the sound in this way.

When we say words, the vowel sounds (V) are the ones that usually appear in the middle, and the consonant sounds (C) at the edges, like this:

pig man cups string

CVC CVC CVCC CCCVCC

We'll be talking a lot about consonants and vowels in later chapters.

CHAPTER 6

Discovering grammar

It must be quite a magical moment when a child realizes that, if sounds are strung together in a certain way, things start to happen. Say 'dada', and the man talks to you. Say 'mama', and the woman does. Say 'bye-bye', and people wave at you. Say 'all gone', and someone takes your dish away or gives you some more to eat. Say 'night-night', and people give you kisses.

Once children have worked out that words are interesting and useful, the floodgates open. By 18 months, most have learned to say about 50 words. What are they talking about, these tiny language-users?

They talk about what's going on around them – what's happening in the 'here and now' – using words like the following (of course, they won't all be pronounced perfectly at this age):

- words to talk about people, such as the members of their family as well as visitors – 'dada', 'grandma', 'Tom', and 'milkman'.
- words to talk about the events of the day, such as 'hello', 'night-night', 'all gone', and 'fall down'.
- words to talk about the actions that people do, such as 'kiss', 'tickle', and 'go' – and also the main words that *stop* actions happening: 'no' and 'don't'.
- words to talk about food, such as 'milk', 'juice', 'drink', and

'din-din'.

- words for parts of the body, such as 'nose' and 'toes', and what some of those body-parts do, such as 'wee-wee'.
- words for clothing, such as 'hat', 'nappy' (or 'diaper' in America), and 'pyjamas' (usually pronounced 'jamas' at this age).
- words for animals, including the really exciting ones seen on the television or a DVD, such as 'dog', 'bird', and 'Tigger'; they are often made child-friendly by adding an extra bit – 'doggie', 'birdie', 'kitty', and 'moo-cow'.
- words for vehicles, another highly exciting world, such as 'car', 'tractor', 'train', and 'bus', and not forgetting unusual means of transport, such as 'wheelbarrow' (pronounced 'eeba' by my son Steven at that age).
- words for toys and games, such as 'ball', 'book', and 'clap-hands'.
- words for household objects, such as 'cup', 'light', and 'spoon' – and especially those which make a noise, such as 'clock' and 'hoover'.
- words for identifying locations, such as 'where', 'there', and 'look', and the very important 'in' and 'on'.
- words for describing things, such as 'big', 'hot', and 'yum-yum'.
- words which show you're taking part in a conversation, such as the reply-words 'yes' and 'ta'.

This is a pretty impressive range of vocabulary for someone who didn't have any words at all six months before. It shows how, once the vocal organs are mature enough to cope, babies rapidly put them to use to talk about the world.

It's the speed of learning that impresses me most. If children have an active vocabulary of around 50 words at 18 months, that means they must have been coming out with a new word, on average, every three or four days! And they understand many more words than that. Their passive vocabulary which I talked about at the end of Chapter 3 is probably three or four times larger. Children understand an awful lot of what is being said around them.

But there's a limit to what you can say, if you're restricted to saying just one word at a time. It's virtually impossible to have a sensible conversation if all you have available are one-word sentences. It makes a good party game, actually. Two people have to talk about a topic, such as where they went on holiday, but they're only allowed to say one word each ('Holiday?', 'France', 'Weather?', 'Lovely'). It gets tricky very quickly, as the sentences they really want to say (such as 'What did you do?' and 'We had a great hotel just by the beach') are banned.

Young children evidently begin to feel the need to say more complicated things at around 18 months, because that's the age when they start joining words together. They stop saying 'gone' and start saying 'teddy gone', 'juice gone', 'daddy gone'. They no longer say 'milk' but start telling us things about the milk – 'milk there', 'milk gone', 'milk cup' (meaning 'the milk is in the cup').

Adults are really rather pleased when children reach this stage, because communication has been a bit hit-and-miss previously. Here's the sort of thing that happens. I remember, when my daughter Sue was about 16 months, she came toddling into the sitting room holding a favourite teddy bear. She stood in front of me and said 'push'. I thought for a moment what she might mean, and then gave her a playful push. That wasn't right. She put on a cross face and said 'No! Push'. So I made another guess, and said: 'Come on, then. Give me a push', and I waited. That wasn't right either. 'No!! Push!'

I was at a loss, and she could see it, so she took me by the hand and brought me into the other room, where there was a toy swing. She put her teddy on the seat and turned to me. 'Push!' So that was it. I had to push teddy on the swing.

'Why didn't you tell me that at the beginning?' I asked her, and got a cold stare for my pains. I know what she was thinking. It was something like this: 'Look, I'm not even one-and-a-half yet, and I only know how to say single-word sentences. I haven't learned much grammar! Give me a break!'

Certainly, to make it clear what she wanted to say, she would have had to know a bit more grammar than she already had. If she'd meant my first guess, she should have said something like 'push me' or 'you push me'. If she'd meant my second guess, she should have said 'me push' or 'me push you'. As it was, she meant to say 'you push teddy' – or even, 'come with me into the other room and give teddy a push on the swing'.

All this was well beyond her, at 16 months. But things would soon change. A few months later she would be able to say 'push me'. Soon after age two she would be able to say 'you push teddy'. And the long version? That would come sometime after her third birthday, once she'd learned to handle such important linking words as 'and'.

So what is this grammar she is discovering? What is grammar? Think about 'push' again, for a moment. What was wrong with that? It didn't make sense. I understood what the word meant, but I couldn't see what she was getting at. So that's the first big thing we have to appreciate about grammar. Grammar is the way we make sense of words. Without grammar, there's only vagueness.

The trouble with words is that most of them have got more than one meaning – they're *ambiguous*. We can see this straight away if we look in a dictionary. Most of the entries give more than one meaning for a word. Take a word like 'band'. We might think its meaning is obvious: 'a pop group'. But that's only one of the meanings of 'band'. It could just as easily refer to a group of marching musician soldiers. Or a group of soldiers or outlaws, such as those who followed Robin Hood. Or a piece of elastic used for holding things together. Or a flat strip of material forming part of a dress or a hat. If we look the word 'band' up in a dictionary, we'll find it has about a dozen meanings. How do we know which is which?

The answer is simple. We put the word into a sentence. And we use the grammar of the sentence to tell us what the word means. For example:

- The newsreader on the television tells us: 'Soldiers were fighting a band of rebels in the south of the country.' That has to be the 'group of outlaws' meaning. It couldn't possibly mean a pop group.
- The DJ on the radio says: 'The band has a new single out

this month.' That has to be the pop group.

- The lady in the shop offers us a choice: 'You can have the jacket with a red band on the sleeve or a green one'. That has to be the strip of material.

In each case, the other words in the sentence help us to work out which meaning of 'band' is the right one.

That is what sentences are for. They help us to make sense of words. Without sentences, what we say simply won't make sense. Little children have to learn that lesson. And so do we, if we want to understand how language works. We need to learn all about the ways our language allows words to come together in sentences. Some ways are possible:

The poodle chased the cat.

And some aren't:

Poodle cat the the chased.

Changing the *order* of the words can change the meaning:

The cat chased the poodle.

And changing the *endings* of words can change the meaning too:

The poodl<u>es</u> chased the cat<u>s</u>.

There are hundreds of ways of building sentences out of words, and children have learned most of them by the time they go to school. They can make sentences that describe events, ask questions, give commands, and do all sorts of other things. They can join them together to tell stories, hold conversations, and send text messages. Without sentences, they'd be lost.

So, when we study a language, we need to work out how its sentences are built. Each language does it in a different way. Some languages, such as French, change the endings of words more than English does. Some languages, such as Chinese, don't have endings like English at all. Some languages, such as Welsh, put the words in a different order.

If we want to understand how people express their ideas and understand each other, then we need to study the way they build their sentences. And the study of the structure of sentences is what we call grammar.

PLAYING WITH GRAMMAR

One of the easiest ways of making a joke is to take a word and use grammar to play with its meaning. Comedians and TV sitcoms do this all the time. They say something which makes you think of a word in one way, and then the next sentence does something totally different. We get a surprise, and that makes us laugh. Here's an example.

Soldiers were fighting a band of rebels in the south of the country. They didn't like their last album.

There's no limit to the number of jokes waiting to be told in this way. (I'm not saying they're good jokes, mind!) Here's the opening line of another one. You can make up whatever punchline you like.

Sharon had a bright green band on her hat. It …

CHAPTER 7

Having a conversation

Why do we need sounds, and words, and sentences? By the time children reach five, they've been alive for over 40,000 hours, and spent a fair bit of that time learning how to speak. They've mastered all the sounds in their language, hundreds of ways of making sentences, and thousands of words. Millions of children have done the job two or three times over, because they've grown up speaking more than one language. Why? What is all that language for?

We use language for all sorts of reasons, but the chief one undoubtedly is so that we can talk to each other. We use it to have a chat, play a game, catch up on the news, tell jokes, ask for help, call each other names, and do a thousand other things. None of this could happen without language. The ordinary, everyday use of language is to have conversations with each other.

Having a conversation seems like the most natural thing in the world. We don't think twice about it now. But it wasn't always that way. We had to learn how to do it. We had to learn the rules.

What's the most basic rule of having a successful conversation? We take turns. I speak and then you do and then I do and then you do. We don't speak at the same time. In an argument, we do sometimes hear a lot of people speaking at once. But once things settle down, everyone takes turns again.

This is especially important if there are several people taking part in a conversation. Imagine: you're in the street talking to three other people about the latest James Bond film. Everyone has got something to say about it. If it's going to be a successful conversation, then all four of you need to get the chance to have your say. If that happens, everyone's happy.

If that doesn't happen, you can end up feeling quite cross. Imagine again: one of the others goes on and on, and doesn't let you get a word in. It's called 'monopolizing the conversation'. Or, when you start to say something, one of the others interrupts you and won't let you finish. Some people are always interrupting. Men seem to interrupt women more than the other way round.

Turn-taking doesn't come naturally. We have to learn how to do it. And babies start that learning process very early on, during the first year of life. They hear their mother talking … they coo or babble … the mother responds … they coo or babble again … the mother responds again. Listen – speak – listen – speak – listen. That's the basis of any conversation. We have to learn to be listeners as well as speakers.

During the second year of life, conversations become more advanced. With a bit more language available, they start to have a more predictable shape. Here's one between Sue and her dad, when she was coming up to age two. They were looking together at a picture in a book. 'What's that?' asked her dad. 'Dog,' she replied. 'Yes, that's a dog,' he said. 'It's a big brown dog, isn't it.' 'Yes,' said Sue. And then she added 'brown dog' – making a brave effort to pronounce the new word (which came out as 'bown').

Let's analyse this little exchange. It's a mini-conversation, in five parts. First, dad asked a question, and Sue replied. Dad then agreed – but notice how he did it. He could just have said 'Yes', and stopped there. But he didn't. He took Sue's little one-word sentence and put it into a bigger sentence of his own: 'that's a dog'. By doing this, he was showing Sue how to take a word and build it into a sentence. Sue would start building sentences like that herself before too long.

But her father didn't stop with just one sentence. He added

another, drawing Sue's attention to some other things about the dog: he was big and brown. Again, he didn't have to say such things. So why did he? The answer is clear from what Sue said next. This was the first time she'd tried to say the word 'brown'. She wouldn't have bothered if she hadn't heard her father say it. He had taught her this word without either of them realizing it.

Conversations between parents and their two-year-old children are usually like that. The parents are continually presenting them with sentences that are a bit more complicated than the ones the children are saying by themselves. The parents are acting like teachers, really.

Another year on, and the conversations go in a fresh direction. Here's Sue talking to her father when she was three-and-a-half. 'Can I have a biscuit?' she asked. And her father then did something which seems strange at first. He got the biscuit and held it out to her, but didn't give it to her. Then he said, 'Can I have a biscuit . . . ?' with a questioning tone of voice. Sue cottoned on immediately. 'Can I have a biscuit, please!' she said. 'Good girl,' said her father, giving her the biscuit. Adding 'ta' for good measure.

What's he doing? Now he's teaching Sue how to carry on a *polite* conversation. Children have to learn about saying 'please' and 'thank you' ('ta', to begin with), and this is done by the parents saying the words over and over until the child picks them up. It takes quite a while, but by age four most children have learned some basic linguistic manners.

Children have to learn all sorts of things about how to talk politely to other people. They have to learn to say 'Hello' and 'Goodbye', 'Good morning' and 'Good night'. They learn to call adults 'Mr' and 'Mrs'. When somebody sneezes, they learn that you should say 'Bless you!' And they learn that, when they hurt themselves or get angry, there are certain 'naughty words' that they're not supposed to say – or, at least, not in their parents' hearing!

Children also have to learn to listen. And that means much more than staying quiet and paying attention. When two people are having a conversation, one is talking and the other is listening. But the listener isn't being silent and still. On the contrary, listeners are always active. They nod or shake their heads, make their faces show agreement or disagreement, make noises such as 'mhm' or 'tut, tut', and say such words as 'yes', 'gosh', or 'no, really?' What they're doing is giving the speaker some *feedback*. They're letting the speaker know that they've understood what is being said to them. It's extremely important to do this. Speakers need to know that they're getting through to their listeners. If they don't get any feedback, they aren't able to carry on talking.

Little children don't give this kind of feedback. That's why we sometimes can't tell, when we're talking to young children, if what we've said has gone in or not. It's something children learn to do, gradually, as they get older. A sign that they've reached conversational maturity is when they actively cooperate with speakers while listening in this way.

Another feature of conversation that children have to learn is 'how to read between the lines' – that is, how to work out what people really mean by the words they use. People don't always say what they mean, especially when they're trying to be polite. Imagine me in a room standing by an open door, and it's a bit cold. Someone might say to me, 'Would you close the door, please?' (if they're being polite) or just 'Shut the door' (if they're not). But think of some of the other ways they might try to get me to shut the door:

'It's getting cold in here.'
'Gosh, there's a draught.'
'Brrrr.'

Why do they say things like this? Probably because they're worried I might think them rude if they asked me directly to shut the door. By being indirect, and letting me know their feelings, they're leaving it up to me whether I shut the door or not. It's their way of being polite. And if I'm being sensitive to their feelings, I will, indeed, go and shut the door.

Children have to learn about all this too. And it takes a while. I remember once, in a primary school, a teacher said to a child (of about seven), 'James, there's a piece of chalk on the floor'. James looked down, saw the chalk, and said 'Yes miss, I can see it' – and left it there. That wasn't the answer the teacher expected! 'Well, pick it up, then!!' she exploded. James soon learned to read between the lines.

STRANGE CONVERSATIONS

People sometimes talk to themselves – or to their plants, or their dishwasher (especially when it goes wrong), or to nothing in particular. Children talk to their toys. Three-year-olds can keep up an imaginary conversation for ages. Mothers often hear the way they talk to their children repeated in the language the children themselves use when talking to their toys. It can be very embarrassing.

These days computer technology allows us to have a conversation with various pieces of equipment, such as a hands-free telephone set in a car, or a washing machine. The machine recognizes our voice (as long as we speak clearly) and performs the action. 'Cool wash at 30 degrees,' we command – and it does it.

With satellite navigation in cars, it's the other way round: the equipment talks to us. 'Drive five point three miles, then turn left,' says the lady in the machine. It's very difficult not to talk back to her. 'Yes, ma'am,' I usually reply – unless she tells me to go in a direction I know would be crazy. Then she gets a telling-off.

CHAPTER 8

Learning to read and write

I ended the last chapter by talking about James having to learn 'to read between the lines'. He wasn't reading, of course; he was listening. That expression is an interesting example of the way we sometimes use the written language to help us talk about what's going on in speech. It's difficult to see many of the sounds that we speak, as I pointed out in Chapter 5. But it's easy to see the marks that we write. They are there, on page and screen.

Children learn about reading very early on – if they're fortunate enough to be growing up in a part of the world where books and screens surround them. Many parents read stories to their children before they are even two years old. Some have their child on their knee as they surf the internet. I know a two-year-old who had learned to identify some of the letters on the computer keyboard and could press them upon request. I wouldn't be surprised to find a two-year-old texter out there somewhere!

If children are exposed to books, they soon learn the basic facts of life about reading. They work it out that books have pages, and that pages have to be turned in a certain order. In some languages, such as English, people turn the pages from right to left. In others, such as Arabic, they turn them from left to right. They learn that books have to be held in a certain way – that pages (and especially pictures) look odd if they're upside-down. And they quickly find pictures fascinating, especially of things they know about from their own world, such as people and animals and cars.

They also notice the little black squiggles that fill a lot of the page. And as they get older, they realize that these are the important bits. If a story is really exciting, it dawns on them that this is because the reader is somehow managing to extract the excitement out of these black marks. Here too there are rules to be learned. The squiggles are organized in lines, and these have to be read (in English) from top to bottom, and from left to right. Children exposed to books written in Arabic or Chinese have to learn that reading goes in other directions.

It doesn't take them long, either, to realize that a book stays the same, each time it's read. As a result, after repeated reading, they come to know a favourite story off by heart. Woe betide the parent who decides to leave out a page or two before bedtime! Once, after a tiring day, I was telling a bedtime story and tried to shorten the story of 'The Three Little Pigs' by going straight from the house of straw to the house of bricks. I thought it wouldn't be noticed if I made it 'The Two Little Pigs'. Not a chance. I got a severe telling-off, and had to start the story all over again, paying special attention to the house of twigs.

We sometimes don't realize just how much exposure children get to the written language around them. They see it everywhere – on shop signs and billboards, in supermarkets, on the front and sides of buses, on newspapers and envelopes, on the tins and bottles in kitchen cupboards, in television commercials and film credits, and, of course, on computer screens and mobile phones. Not surprisingly, then, many three- or four-year-old children have worked out what's going on, and it's possible to carry out some simple experiments to show this.

Collect a few pictures of objects, some of which have writing on and some which don't. An example of the first would be a bus with a number on the front and the name of the company along the side, or a shop with a name above the window. An example of the second would be a countryside scene or a group of people standing around. Then ask the child to look at each picture and 'show me something that you can read'. Many young children can do this, even before they can actually read anything themselves.

We can do a similar experiment with pictures like these: a woman looking at a newspaper, a man digging a garden, a boy sending a text, and a girl riding a bike. This time we ask: 'Show me someone who's reading.' If the children are at the stage of being ready to read, they will point to the woman and the boy.

The next bit is the tricky bit – recognizing the different marks on the page. In English, there are letters and punctuation marks to be learned. In Chinese and Japanese, there are pictorial signs to be learned. That's quite unusual in English, which has only a few picture signs – such as £, & and @.

English – like most other languages – is written using an alphabet. 'Alphabet' is a word which comes from the names of the first two letters in the Greek system of writing: 'alpha' and 'beta'. In an alphabet, a letter stands for a sound. So, letter <b> stands for sound [b]. Letter <s> stands for sound [s], and so on. Notice how we need to use different kinds of brackets to show whether we're talking about a letter or a sound.

In an ideal alphabet, each letter stands for just one sound. That's called a 'phonetic alphabet', and languages which have phonetic alphabets are very easy to read. English, unfortunately, isn't like that. The English alphabet has 26 letters, but there are over 40 sounds in English speech. This means that some letters stand for more than one sound. How do you pronounce the letter <o>, for instance? It all depends. Say these words and you'll see: 'got', 'go', 'son', 'woman', 'women'. Sometimes it's very short, as in 'got'. Sometimes it's long, as in 'go'. Sometimes it even sounds like an [i], as in 'women'.

It gets worse. Sometimes two letters stand for one sound. Make the sound which tells someone to be quiet. If we write it down, we have to use two letters: 'sh'. Or more than two, if we make a really long shushing noise: 'shhhh'. And we can add an exclamation mark if we want to show that we're saying it really loudly: 'sh!' That's quite a lot to learn. But there are still more possibilities. We could write it 'Sh!', with a capital letter. Or 'SHHH!', all in capitals. Or we could turn it into a word, and write 'Shush'.

Capital letters add an extra complication. Although there are 26 letters in the English alphabet, when we write them down it turns out that there are 52, because each letter appears in two forms. We have 'big A' and 'little a', 'big B' and 'little b', and so on. Printers don't use words like 'big' and 'little'. Big letters are called 'upper-case', or 'capital', letters. Little letters are called 'lower-case' letters. These terms come from the days when printers used to keep the letters they needed for printing in two large boxes, or 'cases'. The different capital letters were held in compartments in the top box, or 'upper case'; the small letters were held in the lower box – the 'lower case'.

And there's one more complication. Each of these letters, upper-case or lower-case, can appear in a number of different shapes. Here are just some of the ways you might see letter <A> appearing in a magazine or on a computer screen:

A, **A**, **A**, 𝔄, 𝒜, **A**, **A**, A, 𝒜

These are all from different printing designs, called *typefaces*. We gradually learn to recognize that, despite all the differences, what we have here is the single letter 'A'. But to begin with, these differences can get in the way of learning to read.

However, despite all these difficulties, most children do learn to read well after a couple of years. Parents often teach them the letters of the alphabet before they get to school. Many have practised writing a few letters, such as the letters of their name. To begin with, they think that the letters mean their name. 'L' means 'Lucy'. 'M' means 'Mateo'. And letters take on other meanings too. 'X' means 'kiss'. 'K' means 'cornflakes'. 'P' means 'Parking'. 'M' means 'McDonalds'.

It's a short step from here to reading sequences of letters, such as 'Ben' or 'Dad', and saying them at the same time. Children learn that 'words' are things that have spaces on either side. And they notice the shapes of some of these words standing out on the page. In reading about Winnie the Pooh, for example, many children can point to such names as 'Pooh', 'Tigger', and 'Owl', when asked to do so, even though they can't read the other words on the page.

Then, the breakthrough. They work out that the sequence of letters <d> + <o> + <g> corresponds to the sequence of sounds they make when they say [dog]. And they discover that most words are like this. Not all. Awkward words like 'the' and 'cough' have to be learned in a different way, off by heart. But words like 'cat' and 'top' and 'swim' and 'strong' and 'tomato' can be sounded out letter by letter. And, after they've twigged that two letters sometimes stand for a single sound, they can sound out 'tree' and 'look' and thousands more words. Eventually, they won't need to sound out words letter-by-letter any more. They become fluent readers.

But 'sounding out' is a skill we never lose. It's something we all do when we meet a new long word. Here's an example. Try saying out loud the long form of the word 'DNA', which is an important concept in biology: 'deoxyribonucleic acid'. The only way to do this is to go through it slowly, bit by bit – 'de – oxy – ri – bo – nu – cle – ic'. Then have a go at saying it all at once. After a few goes, you'll be able to say it without thinking.

Some children work all this out for themselves, and end up reading simple stories before they get to school, and even writing short words. But for most, learning to read and write takes place in school. And it's usually in school that some children discover that they have a special problem in learning to read. They find it difficult to grasp the relationship between sounds and letters. They can't hold in their minds the order in which the letters appear on the page. Even after trying very hard, a page still looks to them like a jumble of squiggles. Children who feel like this have *dyslexia*, and they need extra help to get over the problem.

Once we've learned to read and write, we're said to be *literate*. People who haven't learned to read and write are called *illiterate*. There are millions of people around the world who are illiterate. They haven't been able to learn, perhaps because there was no school nearby when they were young, or perhaps the school had few books or writing materials. Even in such countries as the UK and the USA, a surprising number of people either can't read or have great difficulty in reading. And virtually everyone who speaks English sooner or later comes up against the problem of spelling. Why is English spelling such a nightmare?

SPECIAL LETTERS

How do you learn to read and write if you're blind? One of the most widely used methods is called *braille* (pronounced 'brayl'), named after the person who invented it at the beginning of the nineteenth century, Frenchman Louis Braille. In its most basic form, each letter is shown in a rectangular cell by a cluster of raised dots that can be felt with the finger tips. There are special shapes for numbers too, and for punctuation marks and letters with accents (in languages like French).

In a more developed version, there are shapes for some words – very frequent words, such as 'and', 'you', and 'have' – and parts of words, such as 'ing' (as in 'jumping' and 'going'). This saves a lot of space, especially in places where there isn't much room, such as on public signs or restaurant menus.

There are six possible dots available in each cell, and the black dots show the ones that are raised. For English, they are usually set out in two groups of 10, and a final group of six. If you look carefully, you'll see that K to T is the same as A to J, but with an extra dot at the bottom. U, V, X, Y and Z are the same as A to E, but with two dots at the bottom. W is the odd one out – because French didn't use that letter in its alphabet at the time when Braille devised his system.

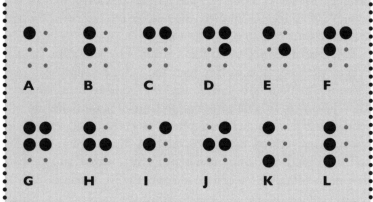

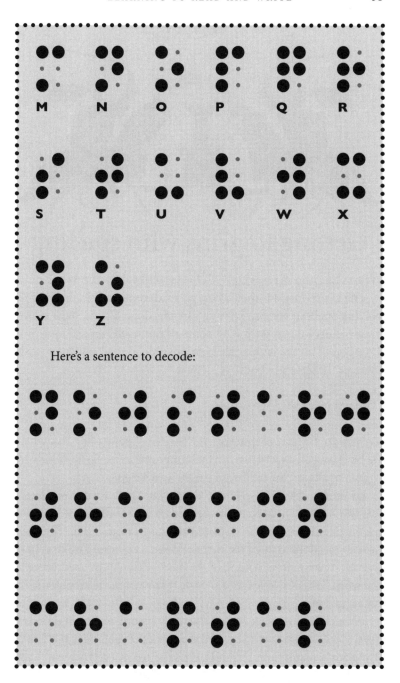

Here's a sentence to decode:

CHAPTER 9

Getting to grips with spelling

We can be good readers and still find spelling difficult. Why?

The main reason is that, when we read, someone else has sorted out the spelling for us. They've already done all the hard work. That means we can skim over some of the words and not pay full attention to all the letters. It's even possible to read sentences with some of the letters left out.

I xpct yu cn read ths sntnce.

Texters do this sort of thing, as we'll see (in Chapter 30). But when we have to spell a word, we can't take any shortcuts. Spellers have to come up with *all* the letters, to get the word right.

It's quite tricky. If somebody asks us to spell a word out loud, just think what we have to do. Let's say it's 'TOMATOES'. First we have to hold the spoken form of the word in our head. Then we have to recall the written form of the word – assuming we've seen it written down before. And then we have to think our way through the word, letter by letter, and say the names of the letters aloud, in the right order.

If we can't remember seeing the word before, we've got an extra job to do. Now we have to try and work out the spelling in our head, using our sense of how it sounds. If it's spelled in a regular way, we'll probably get it right. But people don't usually ask us to spell easy words. They go out of their way, especially in competitions, to find the hard ones – horrors like 'accommodation' and 'bureaucratic' and 'rhinoceros'.

Anyone who's been in a spelling competition knows how easy it is to get things wrong. We might know the spelling of a word, but in the panic to get it right we say the wrong letter, or get the letters mixed up. Out comes T – O – M – A – T – E – O – S. We've been so anxious to remember that there's an E at the end that we say it too soon! It's no good complaining to the judge. With spelling, we've got to get things right first time.

Why do we need to get our spellings right? Because, for the past 300 years or so, spelling has become part of the way that people make judgements about us. If we don't spell correctly, we give the impression that we're ignorant, or careless, or lazy. It can make all the difference. If two people are applying for a job, and one fills in the application form in correct spelling, and the other doesn't, who do you think will get the job?

Getting the spelling right is also important when we use the internet. If we spell an electronic address wrongly, we won't reach the site we want. And if we're looking something up on one of the search engines, and misspell the search words, we can end up with all kinds of rubbish. A search engine like Google is very clever, as it notices common misspellings and asks us to check our typing. The other day I wanted some information about Florida and typed in 'Flordia' by mistake. 'Did you mean Florida?' it asked me. Oops, yes. Thank you very much.

Most computers come armed with a spelling checker, and this can sometimes be helpful if we type something incorrectly. The wrong word is highlighted on our screen in some way, such as with red underlining. But we should never rely completely on a spelling checker. It will flag up words only if they don't exist in the dictionary. If our spelling mistakes look like real words, the checker won't point them out. An American professor, Jerrold Zar, once wrote a poem called 'An Ode to a Spellchecker', and it starts like this:

Eye halve a spelling check her
It came with my pea sea.
It plane lee marks four my revue
Miss steaks aye kin knot sea.

No computer spellchecker would see anything wrong with that.

If our spelling is careless, all kinds of things can go wrong. Not only will we not find our way around the internet, we'll find it difficult to send clever text messages. If it's 'cool' to leave letters out, when we text, then we have to know the letters are there in the first place! The best texters are always the best spellers. Or think about the way we sign up for sites that ask us for a user name and password. Get the spelling wrong, and we won't be allowed in. It pays us to make the effort to spell as well as possible.

There are very few places where people don't mind if we spell things wrongly. We can get away with some strange spellings when we're chatting online in one of the social networking sites, such as Facebook or Twitter, or having an instant messaging exchange, or texting, or emailing. But even there we have to be on our guard. If our spellings are too bizarre, others simply won't understand what we're saying.

That's the reason standard spelling developed in the first place, of course. If we all spell in the same way, then we'll understand each other's writing. If we all use our own personal spelling system, we won't. In the Middle Ages, there was no standard spelling. People spelled words more or less as they liked, making them reflect the way they sounded in their speech. Somebody from the north of England would spell words one way, reflecting their northern accent; somebody from the south would spell them a different way, reflecting their southern accent. People would also have their own favourite spellings. But nobody bothered much about being consistent. In medieval manuscripts, we often find the same word spelled in different ways in the same line. Not even personal names were spelled consistently. There are six signatures thought to be written by Shakespeare himself. They include the spellings

'Shaksper', 'Shakspere', and 'Shakspeare'.

Things changed in the eighteenth century, when a new mood swept through society. Spelling became one of the ways in which people could tell an educated person from an uneducated one. And from then on, in English schools, children had to get their spellings right. They would take lists of spellings home each day to be learned, and be tested on them the next day. Generations of children had correct spellings beaten into them!

Why is English spelling so difficult? It's because of all the different influences the language has had, over the past thousand years. English was first written down by monks in Anglo-Saxon times, around the seventh century, and they did the best they could, trying to make the spellings closely reflect the sounds. For example, the word for 'queen', which – if we listen carefully – has four sounds, was usually spelled with four letters, most often as 'cwen'. But that changed after the Norman Conquest in 1066. French writers came to Britain, and they brought with them their own favourite ways of spelling words. One of these was the use of <qu>. And they began spelling the long vowel sound as <ee>.

Hundreds of words were respelled in this way. That's where the <gh> in the word 'night' comes from. And why do we spell 'circle' and 'cell' with a <c> and not an <s>? The French started that too.

And the <gh> in 'ghost'? That was simply a <g> in Anglo-Saxon times. The French aren't to blame for that. This time the change came from a different part of the world: Belgium and Holland. When a Londoner called William Caxton set up his printing press in 1476, he employed people from northern Europe, where he had learned his trade. They brought in some of their own favourite spellings, and <gh> was one of them. The word 'ghost' was 'gheest' in Dutch.

Once book printing started, the spelling of many words became fixed. That's the good news. The bad news is that people gradually changed the way they spoke, so that eventually spelling stopped reflecting their pronunciation. In Anglo-Saxon times, people pronounced the <k> in such words as 'know' and 'knight', and they carried on doing it into the Middle Ages. So Caxton naturally printed these words with a <k>. But then they stopped pronouncing the <k> (we'll see why in a later chapter), giving us the pronunciation that we still have today. It would have been nice if the spelling had changed to reflect the new pronunciation, but this didn't happen. Caxton's spelling stuck. And today, we have to learn the 'silent letters' in many words like those.

A little later, in the sixteenth century, more silent letters crept in. A number of writers thought it would be helpful if English spelling showed readers where words came from. Take a word like 'debt'. We pronounce it [det] – and that's how it was spelled in the Middle Ages. We find such spellings as <det> and <dett>. So where did the <b> come from? 'Debt' comes from a Latin word, 'debitum'. Writers added the <b> in order to give a hint about the word's origins, and the practice caught on. We all spell it that way now.

Over the next 400 years, people from Britain travelled all over the world, bringing back new objects, experiences, ideas – and words. New words arrived from many languages, such as Portuguese, Italian, Arabic, and Chinese, and people had to decide how to spell them. Some very strange-looking spellings were the result – spellings that had never been seen in English before. Here's a small selection:

grotesque, pizza, gymkhana, karate, tattoo, llama, bazaar, guitar

With some of these words, it took quite a long time before people decided which was the best way to spell them. Even today, there are some words which writers haven't made up their mind about. Do you eat 'yogurt', 'yoghourt', or 'yoghurt'? You'll find all three spellings these days.

English spelling is complicated, then, because an originally quite simple system has been pulled in many directions over the past thousand years. Some people have tried to reform it, to make it simpler, but never with any great success. So we have to spend a lot of time and energy learning it. But once we do, we have an enormously useful skill at our disposal. We know that we will be able to read anything that people have written in English around the world. And we know that what we write will be readable by anyone else in the English-speaking world. Once everyone learns to spell in the same way, it makes the task of communication very much easier. Indeed, it is the foundation of some ways of communicating. Without a standard spelling system to rely on, the internet would collapse.

SPELLING PLAYTIME

Once a standard spelling system exists, people can play with it to make special effects. We find stores spelling their names in distinctive ways, such as QuikTrip, SuperValu, and Toys 'R' Us (often seen with the 'R' back to front). Many products have special spellings, such as Nu Skin. And odd spellings are especially common on internet sites, because if we want to make up a new domain name we'll probably find that all the words with normal spellings have already been taken. That's why we see names like Flickr.

Pop groups like to play with spelling too. Here's a small selection:

the Beatles	**Outkast**	**Siouxsie Sioux**
Rob da Bank	**Sugababes**	**the Monkees**
Eminem	**Gorillaz**	**Boyzone**

It's not difficult to make up new names, using this method. Say you start a pop group and think of calling it 'Cool Dudes'. That might sound a bit boring, because 'cool dudes' has been so often used in everyday speech. But once you start playing with the spelling, all kinds of interesting possibilities exist. How about 'Kool Doods'?

The effect only works because we know the 'real' spelling that lies behind it. Anyone who thinks the normal spelling of 'cool' is 'kool' won't get the point. Rappers have to know how to spell too.

CHAPTER 10

Spelling rules and variations

I mentioned 'yogurt', in Chapter 9, because it has more than one spelling. Are there any other words like this? Quite a few, actually.

If we read through the entries in a dictionary, we often find words which can be spelled in more than one way. Most of them are due to differences between British and American English. In the early 1800s, an American dictionary-writer called Noah Webster changed the spelling of certain words to make the English language look more American, and they caught on. So today, when British people read an American newspaper, they notice many differences – as, of course, do Americans when they read a British newspaper.

American English	*British English*
color	colour
center	centre
pretense	pretence
traveler	traveller
jewelry	jewellery
gray	grey
pajamas	pyjamas
tires	tyres

There are lots more.

People who live in parts of the world outside the USA might think that how Americans spell is nothing to do with them. Unfortunately, life isn't so simple! Because the USA has become such a powerful and influential nation, people in Britain, Australia, Canada, and other parts of the world see American spellings all over the place. They see them in films, books, pop songs, and all over the internet. I just typed 'color' into Google and got 867 million hits. Then I typed 'colour' and got 163 million. But, because of the way the software works, when we look down the list of hits we see both spellings.

As a result, over the past 200 years, American spellings have begun to influence the way people spell in other parts of the world. Once, we would have seen only 'encyclopaedias' in Britain, with an <ae> spelling. Today, we more often find 'encyclopedias', with an <e>. That's an American usage which has caught on. When working with computers, most British people use the American spellings 'program', 'hard disk', and 'analog' instead of 'programme', 'hard disc', and 'analogue'.

While Noah Webster was trying to tidy up American spelling, people in Britain were trying to sort out British spelling. In the eighteenth century, lots of words were still being spelled in more than one way, such as 'raindeer' and 'reindeer', 'error' and 'errour', or 'music' and 'musick'. Samuel Johnson compiled a huge dictionary in 1755, and many of his choices of spellings became accepted because the printing-houses used them. For instance, thanks to him, we now spell 'receipt' with a <p> (not 'receit') and 'entire' with an <e> (not 'intire'). On the other hand, not all of his choices were taken up. He wanted all words ending in a <c> to be spelled <ck>, and that definitely didn't catch on. We write 'comic' and 'music' today, not 'comick' and 'musick'.

The way publishers and printers spell words also has a huge effect on whether we think a spelling is correct or not. And even they don't always agree! Pick up a book and you see one spelling; pick up another book and you see a different one. Here are some examples of the differences:

judgment	judgement	
recognise	recognize	
flower-pot	flower pot	flowerpot
biased	biassed	
movable	moveable	
enthral	enthrall	
the equator	the Equator	

Sometimes the spelling we use depends on the meaning. We buy a 'theatre programme' but a 'computer program'.

When you read through a book, you won't notice these variations. That's because a *copy-editor* has gone through the text, before it is published, to make sure that any words with alternative spellings appear in the same form. Say I was writing a novel and I wrote a sentence like this, you'd probably notice there was something odd about it:

I *realised* John was upset and he *realized* I was.

'Can't you make your mind up?' you might well ask. Because both forms exist in English, it's very easy, when you're writing a book – or an essay – to use one spelling and then another. Copy-editors get rid of such inconsistencies. (In this book words like 'realize' will always be spelled with a 'z'.)

So, when people talk about how important it is to use correct spelling, they're right, because if we spelled any old way, we wouldn't get our meaning across. But we also have to recognize that sometimes there's more than one 'correct spelling'. How do we decide which to go for? Most people simply do what their teachers told them to do when they went to school. It's always been that way.

Spelling is just one of the ways where we have to get things right, if we don't want the way we write to be criticized. What are the others?

We need to get the punctuation right as well. This ought to be easy, because there are only a dozen or so punctuation marks to learn – compared with thousands of spellings – but actually there are complications here also. It's not too hard to learn that we need a mark of some kind to show we've reached the end of a sentence. These are the options in English:

Mary went into the garden.
Mary went into the garden?
Mary went into the garden!
Mary went into the garden . . .

And, of course, in really informal writing, such as in a chatroom or an instant message, we can do things like this:

Mary went into the garden!!!!!!!!!!
Mary went into the garden???

Children learn the value of these different marks when they're learning to read, and they usually do so quite quickly because the meaning of each mark is fairly clear. We use a question-mark to ask a question. We use an exclamation-mark when we want to express a strong emotion. We use three dots, or ellipses, when we want to show that a sentence is unfinished. We use a full-stop when we just want to show that a sentence is finished, without adding any special meaning.

Some of the other punctuation marks, though, are more difficult to learn to use. And not everyone agrees how to use them. Take commas. A comma is a useful mark, because it helps us to show which words belong together. If somebody left you a message like this, how many things would you have to buy?

Get some fruit, juice, tomatoes, and eggs.

Four, of course. But how many now?

Get some fruit juice, tomatoes, and eggs.

Now it's three. The comma makes all the difference.

But would it make any difference if you saw this message, with no comma after the word 'tomatoes'?

Get some fruit, juice, tomatoes and eggs.

That makes no difference at all. And when we look at the way such sentences are punctuated in books and magazines, we find that some people do put a comma in before the word 'and' in a list, and some don't.

There's a strong personal element in the way people punctuate their writing. I know one novelist who puts commas in wherever possible. He writes sentences like this:

Fortunately, the bus was on time, so Sheema wasn't late for the concert.

I know another who leaves them out whenever he can. He writes sentences like this:

Fortunately the bus was on time so Sheema wasn't late for the concert.

Some people get very upset about such things. They say: 'You must ALWAYS have a comma after a word like "fortunately".' But not everyone agrees. And we find famous writers doing both.

Whether we do or don't use commas depends on all kinds of things. Sometimes we have no choice in the matter. In modern English, everyone puts commas in here:

They were playing trumpets, clarinets, violins, oboes . . .

and nobody puts a comma in here:

The musicians, went home.

But whether we use commas in examples like the 'fortunately' one depends on how we want the sentence to sound. Adding them can alter the flow or rhythm of a sentence. Some writers spend ages deciding whether to use a comma or not. Playwright Oscar Wilde once said: 'I was working on the proof of one of my poems all the morning, and took out a comma. In the afternoon I put it back again!'

It isn't just English that has rules of spelling and punctuation, and arguments about usage. We find them in every language that's been written down. The rules may not be the same as for English, mind. When we read Spanish, one of the first things we notice is the way questions and exclamations have the marks at the beginning and the end of the sentence – and the ones at the beginning are upside-down:

English	*Spanish*
How are you?	¿Cómo está? (pronounced 'ko̲hmoh esta̲')
What a shame!	¡Qué lástima! (pronounced 'kay la̲steema')

When we write Spanish, we have to learn to follow their rules and not our own.

Even in our own language, we sometimes have to learn new rules, because the system of marks is always developing. The internet, in particular, has introduced some new kinds of punctuation. Look at the way web addresses are written:

http://www.thisisanexample.com/chapter10

If we read that address aloud, we have to say 'dot' and 'forward slash' (or just 'slash'). That's new, in the history of English punctuation.

So there's a lot to learn about spelling and punctuation, and it takes many years to learn all the rules, and all the exceptions to the rules, and all the uncertainties about usage. But once we've done it, we're in a powerful position. We've become a member of a worldwide club of people, all of whom have done the same thing. We know that we'll be able to read what they have written; and we know that they'll be able to read what we write ourselves.

We need a word to summarize that state of affairs, and that word is 'standard'.

What we've done, when we've learned to spell and punctuate, is learn standard English – or standard Spanish, or standard French, or whichever language we happen to be learning. Having a standard way of writing means that people will be able to understand each other. And spelling and punctuation are two of the main means of enabling that to happen.

Two of the main means? That suggests there are others. There are indeed. We have to keep an eye on our vocabulary too. And above all, we have to learn standard grammar.

HOW DO WE SAY @?

In 1971, an American computer engineer called Ray Tomlinson sent the first ever email. He needed a symbol to identify the location of the email sender within the computer system that sends and receives messages, and he chose @ – pronounced 'at'. Today, we call it the 'at sign' in English.

But other languages sometimes give it different names. People look at its funny shape and compare it to all sorts of things, such as a worm, an elephant's trunk, or a monkey's tail. It's called a 'malpa' in Poland (that's the word for 'monkey' in Polish), a 'sobaka' in Russia (the word for 'dog' in Russian), and a 'papaka' in Greece (the word for 'duckling' in Greek). My favourite is one of the names it's received in Finland: 'miukumauku' – Finnish for 'miaow-meow'.

CHAPTER 11

Grammar rules and variations

Grammar, you'll remember from Chapter 6, is the way we build sentences out of words. When we learn to talk, we discover the rules which control the way this is done. In English, we hear lots of sentences like this:

I bought a coat.
Little Johnny broke a window.
The postman delivered some letters.

We can work out that each sentence has three parts. Someone ('I', 'Little Johnny', 'The postman') did something ('bought', 'broke', 'delivered'), and something was affected by the result of that action – 'a coat' was bought, 'a window' was broken, 'some letters' were delivered. Everybody talks and writes like that in English. They have to put the words in that order to be understood. If someone began to say things like this:

Bought a coat I.
A window broke little Johnny.
Delivered the some letters postman.

we'd call for the men in white coats.

Similarly, we learn that the parts of sentences have rules too. We say 'a coat', 'the postman', and 'some letters', not 'coat a', 'postman the', and 'letters some'. We say 'little Johnny', not 'Johnny little'. Everybody agrees about that too.

These are some of the basic rules of standard English. And if we know some grammar terms, we can say what the rules are. 'The' is called the *definite article*. Words like 'postman' and 'window' are called *nouns*. So we can say, 'In English, the definite article always comes before the noun.'

Do all languages have the same rule? Not at all. In some languages, the definite article goes *after* the noun. In Romanian, the word for 'hotel' is the same as English, and the word for 'the' is 'ul'. But if we want to say 'the hotel' in Romanian, we have to say 'hotelul' – 'hotel the'.

The English language has hundreds of rules of grammar whose purpose is to help us say whatever we want. If we want to talk about more than one thing, the language lets us do so by giving us *singulars* and *plurals* – 'egg' and 'eggs', 'mouse' and 'mice'. If we want to describe things, the language gives us ways of *comparing* – 'big', 'bigger', and 'biggest'. If we want to talk about what's happening in the future, the language gives us several choices, each with a slightly different meaning – 'I will go', 'I might go', 'I'm about to go', and so on.

These are all examples where every English language user does the same thing. In other words, they're part of standard English. But every now and again we come across sentences where *not* everyone does the same thing. For instance, how would you express the idea that there's no post office in a village? Here are just a few of the ways:

1. The village does not have a post office.
2. The village has no post office.
3. The village doesn't have a post office.
4. The village hasn't got a post office.
5. The village hasn't got no post office.
6. The village ain't got no post office.

They all say the same thing, but they don't all *feel* the same, do they? Examples 1 and 2 sound rather careful and formal. Numbers 3 and 4 sound a bit more everyday and colloquial. Examples 5 and 6 sound straight off the street.

Which would you see in a newspaper report or hear on the television news? Numbers 1 and 2 are the most likely. We might hear numbers 3 and 4 from a roving reporter who was visiting the village. And we might hear numbers 5 and 6 from the people in the village that the reporter was interviewing. But we'd never see numbers 5 and 6 in a newspaper, unless the reporter was quoting what someone had said. And would we ever hear them coming out of the mouth of a newsreader? Try and imagine it:

> This is the six o'clock news. Thousands of people took to the streets today in the village of Plopton in Yorkshire, protesting about the closure of their local store. The village ain't got no post office, and …

I don't think so.

Usages like 'ain't' and 'hasn't got no' are examples of *nonstandard* English. They're both used by millions of people in their everyday speech, but they aren't felt to be 'good English'. For over 200 years, English-speaking society has lived with the notion that some ways of speaking and writing are 'good' and some are 'bad'. The same point applies to other kinds of behaviour, such as table manners. It's bad manners to put a knife in our mouth. It's bad manners to slurp our soup. It's bad manners to pick our bowl up and suck in the soup. On the other hand, it's good manners if we tip our bowl slightly away from us and use our spoon to eat the soup (quietly).

Why is it 'good' to eat your soup one way and not another? It's just the way things are. Sometime in the dim and distant past it became the fashion, among the most powerful people in society, and it stayed that way. And if we don't want to be criticized, that's how we have to behave.

Why is it 'good' to say 'hasn't got any' and bad to say 'ain't got no'? The same reason. Sometime in the past – during the eighteenth century, to be precise – the most powerful people in society began to speak and write in a way which they felt to be especially elegant. They heard ordinary people on the streets say such things as 'ain't got no', so they decided that they would speak and write differently. Several other kinds of sentence were affected too. No upper-class person would ever say such things as 'I were sat down' or 'We was eating', because that's the way 'ordinary' people spoke.

Well, once the royal family, the aristocrats, the bishops, the professors, and all the other important people chose such patterns as 'does not have any' as their normal way of speaking and writing, there was huge pressure on anybody who wanted to be somebody in society to do the same thing. So a big gap opened up. The upper classes called anyone who used examples 5 and 6 above, or sentences like 'I were sat down', a whole host of bad names – they were 'slovenly', 'ungrammatical', 'careless'. In return, the lower classes called anyone who used examples 1 and 2, or sentences like 'I was sitting down', by a different set of bad names – 'posh', 'affected', 'la-di-da'.

The gap is still there today. Examples 1, 2, 3, and 4 are all considered to be standard English – 1 and 2 being more formal in style, and 3 and 4 more casual. But examples 5 and 6 are considered to be non-standard English. And that means we have to be careful. It's no problem if we use examples like 5 and 6 in the street with our mates. But if we use them in an essay, or in an exam, or while talking in public, or in any other place where people expect us to be on our best behaviour, then we're likely to get some strange looks – and some low marks!

So there's more to standard English than at first meets the eye. It isn't just the kind of English that's most widely understood around the world. It's also the kind of English that's the most useful if we want a good job or an influential position in society. And it doesn't come naturally. We all have to learn to write standard English. That's what happens when we go to school. Also, very few people grow up speaking standard English as young children. They have to learn to speak it – which also happens when they go to school. Outside school, most children speak a kind of English where sentences like examples 5 and 6 are natural. So do their parents and most of the people in their society. You'll hear 'ain't' used throughout Britain, Ireland, the USA, Canada, Australia, South Africa … anywhere, in fact, where English is spoken as a mother tongue.

What happens in school, then, is that children learn there's an alternative way of speaking to the one they use at home and in the street. In former times, teachers would tell them that their home way of talking was 'bad' and that only the standard way was 'good'. That simply gave generations of people inferiority complexes about the way they spoke. Today, most teachers take a more balanced view. They see that both versions have a point.

We need both street grammar and classroom grammar, if we want to handle all the situations that life throws at us. Children will be criticized (by their teachers) if they use street grammar in the classroom, but they'll also be criticized (by their mates) if they use classroom grammar in the street. It's important, then, to understand the differences between the two kinds of language, so that we don't mix them up. Then, once we're in control of them, we can start using them in clever ways, just as we can with spelling and punctuation.

Some newspapers and magazines play with non-standard English. Every now and then we see headlines like this:

WE AIN'T SEEN NOTHING YET

That breaks both the rules of standard English that I've been talking about in this chapter. But we can see immediately that the paper is playing a game with us. The same kind of thing is going on with this one:

IF IT AIN'T BROKE, DON'T FIX IT

Here, as well as 'ain't' the headline-writer is using a non-standard form of 'break'. In standard English, the headline would have read:

IF IT ISN'T BROKEN, DON'T FIX IT

The effect just ain't the same.

I said earlier that most people don't speak standard English at home with their family and friends. What do they speak, then? This is where dialects come in.

THE RETURN OF THE JEDI

Aliens often use non-standard English word order. The best example I know is the Jedi Master, Yoda, in the *Star Wars* films, who speaks a highly unusual form of English. The expected order of the parts of his sentences is back to front.

> Killed not by clones, this Padawan. By a lightsaber, he was.
> To fight this Lord Sidious, strong enough you are not.

It's a clever piece of writing by the scriptwriters. The sentence patterns are quite close to those used in normal English, so we're able to understand them easily. They also have some echoes of English from many centuries ago, so they suit Yoda's great age. But English has never used word orders quite like these, so we get the impression of something totally alien. Which is what Yoda is. Nobody knows where he comes from. In the Star Wars Databank, we are simply told that he is of 'species unknown'.

CHAPTER 12

Accents and dialects

It's one of the first things we notice. We meet someone speaking our language who comes from a different part of the country, or a different part of the world, and we realize that they don't speak it in the same way that we do. They sound different. They use different words and different grammar. The differences may even be so great that we have difficulty understanding them. Why is this?

The answer is all to do with accents and dialects. It's important to understand the difference between these two terms, so I'll take them one at a time.

A *dialect* is a way of talking that belongs to a particular part of a country. It uses local words and phrases, and often these are well known in other parts of the country. For instance, if we heard someone talking about a 'wee child' or a 'bonny coat', we'd be fairly sure they came from Scotland. ('Wee' means 'little' and 'bonny' means 'pretty'.) If we heard someone saying they were running down a 'jigger' or they were wearing a 'cozzy', then the odds are that they're from Liverpool. (A 'jigger' is the alley that runs behind a row of houses; a 'cozzy' is a costume, especially one for swimming.) And someone who says 'nowt' ('nothing') is probably from Yorkshire.

There are more English dialects per square mile in Britain than in any other part of the English-speaking world. This is because Britain has such a varied history, with Germanic people from different parts of Europe settling in different parts of the country, some mixing with Celts from Wales, Scotland, and Ireland. It didn't take long before the settlers in one small locality developed their own special way of talking. But all countries have accents and dialects. In the USA, if we heard someone calling a group of people 'y'all' (= 'you all'), we'd know the speaker came from a southern state, such as Texas, or was copying southern speech. If someone said 'dropped eggs' instead of 'poached eggs', they'd be from the north-east, in New England. And if we sat out on a 'stoop' (the steps leading up to the front of a building) munching on a 'hero' (a type of sandwich), we could be fairly sure of being in or around New York.

Some dialects have hundreds of local words, and many of them have been collected into dictionaries. We often see books of them on sale in tourist centres around the country, and we can find lists of them online too. All we have to do is type 'New York dialect', 'Yorkshire dialect' (or whatever) into a search engine, and we'll get lots of hits. Or we can make up our own lists from the local words we use ourselves. Dialects are always changing, and the words young people use are sometimes different from those used by older people.

Dialects also have distinctive patterns of grammar. For instance, Scots English has its own way of saying 'not'. People who say 'I canna come', 'I'm no going', and 'I dinna ken' are likely to come from Scotland. In standard English, we'd have to say 'I can't come', 'I'm not going', and 'I don't know'. And several local dialects around Britain say things like 'five mile' (instead of 'five miles') or 'I saw thee' (for 'I saw you').

Notice that dialect words and sentences can tell us that someone comes from a particular town or city (such as New York), or a particular county or state (such as Yorkshire or Texas), or a broad part of the country (such as the north-east or Scotland). When we look at the way English is used around the world, we can even talk about whole countries. People talk about 'Australian English' or 'Irish English'. In Chapter 10 I talked about British and American English. Here we have dialect differences on a grand scale.

People in Britain say 'We walked along the pavement'. In most of the USA this would be 'We walked along the sidewalk'. Think of the parts of a car. In Britain we look out through a 'windscreen' at a 'bonnet'; in the USA we look through a 'windshield' at a 'hood'. At the front of a British car there's a 'bumper' and at the back there's a 'boot'; in the USA they are a 'fender' and a 'trunk'. We identify British cars with 'number plates', but American cars have 'license plates'. We switch on our 'sidelights' in Britain, but our 'parking lights' in the USA. Inside British cars there's an 'accelerator', a 'gear stick', and a 'milometer'; inside American cars there's a 'gas pedal', a 'gear shift', and an 'odometer'.

There are also differences in grammar between British and American English. Ask a British person the time at 3.45 and the answer will probably be 'It's a quarter to four'. In many parts of the USA it would be 'It's a quarter of four'. Someone from Britain might say 'I've just got a new coat'. The equivalent American sentence would be 'I've just gotten a new coat'. In Britain, they'd say 'The bus hasn't arrived yet'; in the USA we'd also hear 'The bus didn't arrive yet'.

Dialect differences, then, are all to do with vocabulary and grammar. That's the essential point to remember when thinking about the other important term: *accent*. Accents are only to do with pronunciation. Like dialects, they tell us which part of a country, or which country, someone comes from, but they do it through sounds rather than through words and sentences. All the dialects I've mentioned have an accent. People from Scotland speak in a Scottish accent. People from Liverpool speak in a Liverpool (or 'Scouse') accent. People from America speak in an American accent. And so on.

Actually, we need to be a bit more precise. It's better to say that people from Scotland speak in one of many possible Scottish *accents*. The way they sound in Glasgow is very different from the way they sound in Edinburgh, and people from other parts of Scotland sound different again. It's the same in England, or the USA, or anywhere. There's no such thing as a country with just one accent.

Nor, indeed, is there any such thing as a person with just one accent. Our accent changes over time, depending on where we've lived and who we're talking to. I've lived in Wales, Liverpool, and the south of England, so my accent is a mixture of sounds from all three places. When I'm in Wales, the Welsh bit of my accent comes to the fore. When I visit Liverpool, I sound more Scouse. And when I go to London, I sound more southern.

My accent changes, also, depending on the kind of occasion I'm involved in. If I'm giving a lecture in English to a group of students in Germany, then I'll speak a little more slowly and carefully than usual, and my accent will sound more like someone reading the news on the BBC. And when I'm on the radio myself, the regional features of my pronunciation become less noticeable. Once, someone from my home town, who'd heard me on the radio, stopped me in the street and said 'It didn't sound like you at all!'

But all these accents *are* me. They're all in my head, and my vocal organs can handle each of them. I often unconsciously slip into other accents, too. In fact, everyone does this. You meet someone who has a different accent from your own, and you start getting on well with them. After a while, you'll find yourself talking a bit like they do. And they'll find themselves talking like you do. You end up, both of you, sharing bits of your accents. Then, when you separate, you switch back into your normal accents again.

Why do we have accents? I've said that they tell other people which part of the country we're from. But it's not just which part of the country. Accents can also tell others about the kind of social background we have or the kind of job we do. Listen to the people who read the news on the radio. Sometimes they have a regional accent, and we can tell they come from a particular part of the country. But often they don't. We can hear their accent, and it could be from – anywhere.

In England, that neutral accent is called *Received Pronunciation* – or RP for short. It's an accent that developed at the end of the eighteenth century among upper-class people. You'll remember how, in Chapter 11, I talked about the way these people started to use standard English grammar? That was one of the ways they found to keep their distance from the lower classes, most of whom spoke a regional dialect. Another way was to pronounce their words without any trace of a regional accent. If ordinary people all over the country dropped their 'h' sounds in words like 'hospital' and 'hand', then RP speakers would make sure they kept them in. If ordinary people all over the country pronounced the 'r' in such words as 'car' and 'heart', then RP speakers would make sure they didn't.

As a result, a new kind of accent came into being. At first it was used by the people in powerful positions in society, such as the royal family, bishops, professors, doctors, and judges. Then teachers began to use it in the big public schools (such as Eton, Harrow, and Winchester), and taught it to the children. There are many stories of children with a regional accent arriving for the first time at one of these schools and finding the older children (or even the teachers) laughing at the way they spoke. The newcomers would change their accents to RP within days! That was happening 200 years ago. It still sometimes happens today.

When these children grew up, many of them became lawyers and civil servants, or held other positions of power. Many joined the army or navy and went abroad. The nineteenth century was a time when the British Empire was growing. As new colonies were gained all over the world, British people were put in charge – and they all spoke with an RP accent. Before long, that accent was the 'voice of Britain'. It became the voice of the BBC. And, to this day, the accent that most foreigners are taught, when they learn to speak British English, is RP.

Since 1800, RP has been the chief 'cultured' accent in Britain. A lot of people simply call it 'posh'. It was never spoken by huge numbers – at most, by about five per cent of the population – but it was the accent that people associated with someone who was from the higher social classes or who had received the best education. That's why it was called 'received' pronunciation. It was seen as a sort of inheritance from your ancestors.

Other languages also have cultured accents. There are posh ways of talking in France and Spain, and in any country which has a history of upper-class and lower-class division within society. Other parts of the English-speaking world have their cultured accents too. If you've seen the film *Crocodile Dundee*, you'll have heard Paul Hogan use one of the street accents of Australia. Not everyone in that country speaks like he did. Many Aussies have educated accents too.

Things have begun to change in Britain. The division between upper and lower classes isn't as sharp as it used to be. People with regional accents have obtained some of the top jobs in society. Prime Minister Gordon Brown with a Scottish accent. Huw Edwards reading the BBC news with a Welsh accent. If people telephone a call centre to get information about train times, or how to insure a car, the person on the other end of the phone will very likely have a regional accent these days. Once upon a time, you'd only have heard RP. A few years ago, linguists did a survey of the accents used in call centres in Britain, and they found that Edinburgh and Yorkshire accents were the most popular. And some accents, such as those from Birmingham or Newcastle, were hardly used at all.

People have strong feelings about accents. They think of them as 'beautiful' and 'ugly', 'intelligent' and 'stupid', 'musical' and 'harsh', and much more. But accents can't be classified in this way. What one person hears as melodious, another hears as grating. And some of the accents that are felt to be unpleasant by people inside a country are considered delightful by people outside. The Birmingham accent is often given a low rating by people from England. But when I played several accents to a group of foreigners who didn't know much English, they thought Brummie was one of the most beautiful ones.

Why do we have such strong feelings about accents – and about dialects too? It's all part of a larger story to do with the way language expresses our identity.

WHO'S THERE?

There have always been accents and dialects. The earliest writings in English have differences in spelling, vocabulary, and grammar which show that the authors came from different parts of the country. And if we go back much further, to the time when humans began to talk, we can guess that there would have been accents then too.

Imagine. You're in your cave, and it's a dangerous world outside. You hear a noise, so you call out (in your primitive speech) 'Who's there?' A voice replies. If you recognize the accent of the voice as one that belongs to your tribe, then you'll go outside happily to see what they want. But if you call out 'Who's there?' and you don't recognize the accent, you'd better take your club with you when you go outside, and be on your guard. A strange voice probably means an enemy.

If evolution is a matter of the 'survival of the fittest', then I think accents may have helped. Those who had the best ear for accents may have lived longer. And actually, when you think about it, it's not so different today. I can think of some places where the sound of an alien accent immediately puts people on their guard. Probably you can too.

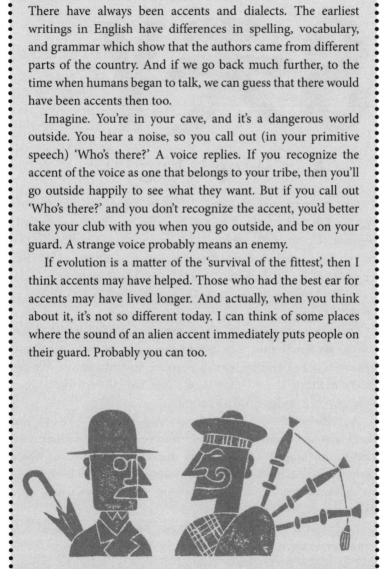

CHAPTER 13

Being bilingual

I know a man from Scotland who's very proud of being Scottish. He wears a kilt, has a tartan hat, and has a badge which says proudly 'I'm from Glasgow'. He obviously has a very strong sense of identity. But he has a problem. If he's round a corner, I can't see his kilt, hat, or badge. If I meet him in the dark I can't see them either. And if he takes all his clothes off to go for a swim, then I've no chance of spotting them.

Question: How can you show someone you're Scottish if you haven't got any clothes or badges to do it with? Answer: By talking. Speech is the one thing we can perceive around corners. We can hear it in the dark. And if the water's cold, we will very likely hear a loud yelp in a strong Scottish accent.

Accents travel easily. They also develop naturally – we can hear them in young children from their third year of life. And they don't cost us anything. We have to buy the clothes and badges which show we're from Scotland, or from Wales, or from New York. When we speak, we don't have to buy anything at all to show where we're from.

And what if someone is from Japan, or Russia, or Brazil? The same points apply. Japanese people can dress up in a Japanese way and do things we associate with Japan, such as eat sushi. But the easiest way to show they're from Japan is to speak Japanese. If accents tell us where people are from, languages do so even more strongly. Fill in the blanks:

> She speaks Danish. She must be from __
> He speaks Polish. He must be from __
> They speak Welsh. They must be from __

It's most likely Denmark, Poland, and Wales.

Notice that if you do this exercise the other way round, the answers become more unpredictable. Try it:

> She's from Wales. So she speaks __

For some, the answer will be Welsh. For others, the answer will be English. And those who speak Welsh could answer 'English' too, because they will all speak both languages – in other words, they're *bilingual*. The term comes from Latin: *bi* means 'two', as in *bicycle* ('two wheels'), and *lingua* is the word for 'language'.

If we speak two languages we're bilingual. If we speak three, we're *trilingual*. If we speak three or more languages, we'd usually be called *multilingual*, though the term *polyglot* is often used. The greatest linguists in the world have learned dozens of languages. Remember Harold Williams, from Chapter 3? He spoke 58!

It's normal for human beings to be bilingual, as we saw when we talked about the way babies easily learn languages. About three-quarters of the human race grows up speaking two or more languages. It's the most natural thing in the world. People use one language at home. They go to the marketplace and speak a different one there. They go to school or church and use another one there. In parts of the world where many cultures meet, the streets are a jumble of different languages, and the people know bits of all of them.

A country usually has a language which most of its people speak – Danish in Denmark, French in France, and so on. But many of those people will also have learned other languages. And many of the people who live there will be immigrants, speaking the language of the country where they were brought up. All countries are multilingual. Some are amazingly so. There are hundreds of languages spoken throughout the USA, for instance.

Even Britain is highly multilingual these days. We often think of England as a monolingual part of the world. But from its earliest times it was multilingual. When the Anglo-Saxons arrived in the country, in the fifth century, they found people speaking Latin (from when the Romans were in Britain) and the various British languages, such as early Welsh and Cornish. Other continental languages were probably spoken in the island too, as a result of trade between Britain and the rest of Europe.

Today, because of huge waves of immigration, especially from the countries of the European Union, the amount of multilingualism in Britain has rocketed. In 1999 there was a survey of the mother tongues of 850,000 children in London schools. It found over 300 languages in use. The most common was English, of course. Next were several languages of people who came from South Asia – Bengali, Panjabi, Gujarati, Hindi, Urdu. Then came two languages from around the Mediterranean – Turkish and Arabic. Then came two languages from Africa – Yoruba (which is spoken in Nigeria) and Somali. Next came one of the languages of China – Cantonese.

I could go on and on, but the point is clear. London is now one of the multilingual capitals of the world, along with New York, Boston, and many other American cities. In half the primary schools in Inner London, over half of the pupils do not speak English as a mother tongue. And in secondary schools the proportion is not much lower – 40 per cent. Those are statistics from 2006. The figures are probably a bit higher now.

London is special, but it's not alone. The national average is six per cent: that is, six out of every hundred children speak a language other than English as their mother tongue. Every large city in the UK contains dozens of languages. And we find them even in smaller towns and villages, because people from abroad have found work there – such as fruit picking, or working in the hotel trade. If you take the boat from Holyhead in North Wales to Dublin in Ireland, you might hear Lithuanian, Polish, and Latvian among the languages of the onboard staff. You might even hear Welsh and

Irish too, if you're lucky. But it's the languages of central Europe you'll hear most often.

Why do people keep their languages like this? Why don't immigrants just drop their old language and learn a new one, when they travel to a new part of the world? Many do just that, of course, as we'll see in a later chapter. But many make every effort to keep their first language alive, speaking it whenever they can, forming local communities where it's used, and teaching it to their children. And the welcoming country often makes every effort to foster multilingualism too, providing services in as many languages as it can afford.

Imagine, if *you* went to live in another country, would you want to leave behind your mother tongue completely? Obviously not. You still have friends and relatives in your old country that you want to talk or write to. And even if you didn't, you have in your head all your knowledge and memories of its culture – the books you read, the pop songs you learned, the slang you picked up. Your mother tongue forms part of your identity – your sense of who you are. And it forms part of the identity of the group of people you know best – those with whom you grew up.

That's why people get very upset when their language is rubbished, or ignored, or – in the worst case – banned. It's not at all uncommon to find governments forbidding the public use of local languages. When General Franco was ruler of Spain, in the 1940s and 1950s, Spanish was the only language allowed in public use. The local languages of Spain, such as Catalan, Basque, and Galician, were repressed. You couldn't even name your child with a local name. Somebody from Barcelona, where Catalan was spoken, might want to call their new babies Beatriu and Lluis, but they would have to adopt the Spanish spellings, Beatriz and Luis. Things are different now.

Every so often we read in the newspapers of people in a country going on a march to support their language. There may even be riots and hunger strikes. It's happened in Quebec, where the French speakers want their language to be given a greater public presence. It's happened in Belgium, where those who speak French and those who speak Flemish are often in conflict. It's happened in Wales and India and several other countries. Why do these things occur? It's because the people feel so strongly about the importance of their language that they're prepared to go to any lengths to preserve it.

One of the most famous such events took place on 21 February 1952 in Dhaka, in what was then East Pakistan. (It's the country of Bangladesh today.) A group of students organized a demonstration to support the use of Bangla as an official language of Pakistan alongside Urdu. The police opened fire, and several people were killed. That moment has not been forgotten. When UNESCO, the United Nations Educational, Scientific and Cultural Organization, decided in 2000 to have an International Mother-Tongue Day, to celebrate all the mother tongues in the world, it chose 21 February.

Anniversaries remind us about the importance of things. That's why we have birthdays and festivals. We don't have many language anniversaries, so it's good to remember them when they do take place. There are just two big days each year: 21 February, and 26 September – the European Day of Languages. They share the same goal: to make people aware of the importance of language diversity and to promote language learning and bilingualism. We'll explore why this is so important in a later chapter.

Bilingualism is a big issue in places like the USA, the UK, and Western Europe. That's because these are places where for centuries most of the people spoke just one language, and saw other languages as inferior. Spanish was the language of Spain; French of France; English of Britain. Any other languages which happened to be spoken in those countries were dismissed as unimportant. They may even have been repressed, as in the case of Franco's Spain. Other countries did similar things. Over a hundred years ago, if you were heard speaking Welsh in a school in Wales, you were punished. The same thing happened if you were caught speaking Breton at schools in Brittany in north-west France. Today, these communities are fighting back, wanting respect for their languages once again. Bilingualism has become a political issue.

The same thing has happened in parts of the world where countries built huge empires. When one country takes over another, the result is usually that the defeated country adopts the language of the invaders and makes it the official language – the one that's used in parliament, the law courts, and the schools. That's why most of the countries of South and Central America use Spanish or Portuguese, why French and English are used in many African countries, and why English is so widespread in North America, southern Asia, Australia, and New Zealand. Bilingualism can be a political issue there too, especially when the new languages threaten the existence of the old ones.

If we want to become multilingual, we have all the world's languages to choose from. But just how many languages are there?

THE EUROPASS

We don't have to be perfectly fluent in different languages to be called multilingual. We might have learned enough just to carry on a basic conversation, or we might only be able to read a language but not speak it. I know several people who can happily chat about everyday matters in various languages, but they wouldn't be able to use them to make a speech or engage in a political debate on TV.

Recognizing a person's different levels of language ability is a major feature of the way people think about languages in Europe these days. An organization called the Council of Europe thought up the idea of a 'language passport', which anyone can fill in. You can see some examples online. Search for *Europass*.

On a Europass we say whether we can just understand a language, or whether we can speak it or write it as well. We say what sort of experience we've had in using our languages, and how well we think we can use them, on a scale from 'basic' to 'proficient'. Someone might have a basic level of Spanish, an intermediate level of French, and an advanced level of English and German, for example.

It's a great idea, as it makes it easier to compare the language skills of people from different countries. I hope, along with our usual passports, we'll all have a language passport one day.

CHAPTER 14

The languages of the world

How many languages are there? Around 6,000. Maybe quite a few more. Maybe quite a few less. It's difficult to be sure.

One reason is that languages are rapidly dying out, in several parts of the world – perhaps as fast as one every few weeks. We'll see in a later chapter why this is happening. But obviously, when languages are disappearing at such a rate, it makes it difficult to arrive at a definite total.

Then there are still a few parts of the world where people are discovering *new* languages. It can happen like this. An expedition travels to an isolated valley in the middle of the forests of Papua New Guinea and finds a small community living there. When they try to talk to the people, they realize that the language isn't like any of the others in the region. The world total of languages goes up by one.

Or this happens. Linguists finally get the chance to investigate the speech of a community living in a coastal village in Indonesia. They assume that the way the people of this village speak is going to be like the way other people speak who live in villages further along the coast – a bit different, perhaps, but not seriously so. In other words, they think the people will just be speaking different dialects of the same language – in much the same way as we find different dialects of English as we move along the coast from Yorkshire to

Lincolnshire. But when the linguists start their study, they discover that the people in the new village speak a totally different language – as different, perhaps, as English is from French or German. It's a big surprise, and the result is that the world total again goes up by one.

This problem of deciding whether a group of people are speaking a *dialect* or a *language* turns up all the time. What's the essential difference between the two? Think it out by exploring the following situation.

There are four men in a room. One is from Liverpool, one is from London, one is from Paris, and one is from Bordeaux. Each speaks only the language of the place where he was brought up. Which of them will be able to understand each other?

The man from Liverpool and the man from London don't speak in exactly the same way, but they'll be able to understand each other most of the time. They'll both say they speak 'English'. And the man from Paris and the man from Bordeaux don't speak in exactly the same way either, but they'll also be able to understand each other most of the time. They'll both say they speak 'French'.

The man from Liverpool and the man from London are speaking different dialects of English. The man from Paris and the man from Bordeaux are speaking different dialects of French. When people speak different dialects, they mostly understand each other.

The two Englishmen will say: 'I don't understand what those other two are saying because I don't speak French.' And the two Frenchmen will say: 'I don't understand what those other two are saying because I don't speak English.' In other words, they realize they're speaking different languages. When people speak different languages, they don't understand each other.

So that's the essential difference between a dialect and a language. A language is made up of many dialects, and the people who speak those dialects generally understand each other (even if they do have the occasional difficulty with local accents or words). Nobody knows just how many dialects there are in the world – at least 20,000, I would say. But they group themselves into about 6,000 languages. We can talk about a family of dialects forming a language. And the story doesn't stop there. Languages form families too.

How can we tell that a group of people belong to the same family? The best evidence is if they look or sound like each other. They've all got big noses or red hair, or they all have deep voices. We can tell that languages belong to the same family in the same sort of way. They look or sound like each other. They have similar sounds, or words, or grammar.

Here's an example. What is the word for 'father' in Spanish? It is 'padre', pronounced something like '<u>pah</u>-dray'. What is the word for 'father' in Italian? Also 'padre', but with a slightly different pronunciation. What is it in Portuguese? 'Pai', pronounced roughly like 'pie' in English. And in French? 'Père', pronounced roughly like 'pear' in English.

We can see more variations when we explore the dialects of a country. If we travel down through Italy, we'll hear several other versions. In Veneto we'll hear 'pare' (pronounced 'pa-ray'); in Milan, it'll be 'pader' (pronounced 'pa-dare'); in Naples it's 'pate' (pronounced 'pa-tay'); and in Sicily 'patri' (pronounced 'pa-tree').

It's easy to see a pattern. All the words begin with a [p] sound. Most of them have a [t] or a [d] in the middle. Most of them have a [r]. And almost all of them have an [a] in the first part and an [e] in the second.

When we see this kind of similarity, we can draw the obvious conclusion. All these words must have a common origin. Once upon a time, there must have been a word – let's think of it as 'pater' – spoken by a group of people. These people then started to move around Europe, and as they did so their speech gradually changed. They developed new pronunciations – new accents, as we called them in Chapter 12. The people who went into Spain changed the [t] into a [d] and altered the order of the sounds, so that [er] became [re]. The people who went into France dropped the [t] altogether, and joined the [a] and [e] into a single long sound, which is written today with an <è> letter.

And this is exactly what happened. We can be definite, for this example, because we know what the historical facts are. There *was* an original word, 'pater'. It was in the Latin language, spoken by the Romans. And we know that the Romans had an empire, and travelled all over western Europe, taking their Latin language with them. Eventually, ordinary people in France, Spain, and other places started to use the word, and changed it in the ways we've seen. The same thing happened to all the other words in Latin. And Latin grammar changed too. The result is the modern languages spoken in these places.

It took several hundred years for all this to happen. Languages change very slowly. But once they do, we end up with a family of languages. Linguists have given a name to the family – in this case, the *Romance* family. And we talk about the *parent* language (Latin) and the *daughter* languages (French, Spanish, Italian, and so on). We also say that French and Spanish and Italian are *sister* languages. It really is a family. And in all, when we include all the local languages and major dialects in France, Spain, and Italy, it's a family that has over 30 members.

All the languages of the world – all 6,000 or so – can be grouped into families like this. The problem is that in many parts of the world there are no historical facts to help us. If we find that some languages in the middle of Africa have similar words, we can draw the same conclusions – but we're often guessing, because we don't know anything about the history of the peoples, or how their languages developed.

In Europe, we're in a very fortunate position, because there are written records for most countries which go back over a thousand years, so we can actually see how the languages have changed over the centuries. Everywhere we notice the same sort of changes in sounds that we saw in the case of the Romance family – a [t] becoming a [d], or an [a] becoming an [e], or the other way round.

The changes always make sense, when we think of how we make sounds. As we saw in Chapter 4, it doesn't take much to change a [t] into a [d]. All we have to do is start the vocal cords vibrating. Nor would it take much to change a [p] into a [f], because these sounds are made in a very similar way. We use two lips to make [p], and we put the bottom lip against the top teeth to make [f].

Then, instead of holding the two lips tightly together, as for [p], we relax the lip a bit and let the air rush through, which produces an [f]. That change from [p] to [f] actually happened in the history of English, as we'll see in a moment.

While the Romans were taking Latin around west and south-west Europe, other groups of people were taking their languages around northern Europe, and changes were taking place there too. In particular, the Germanic people were on the move. They originally lived in the south of Scandinavia, especially in the area where southern Sweden and Denmark are today. Sometime around 1000 BC they started to move south, into central Europe and along the north European coast. Over a thousand years later, some of them arrived in Britain.

As the Germanic people spread around Europe, so their language changed – just as happened in the south with Romance. Today, we call the earliest language of the Germanic people of Scandinavia *Old Norse*. The language of the Germanic people who went into Germany is called *Old High German*. The language of those who went into the north European coast is *Old Frisian*. The language of those who came to Britain is *Old English*.

These people would not have been able to understand the Romans speaking Latin, nor would the Romans have understood the Germanic languages. But when we look at some of the earliest words to be written down in these languages, we find some striking similarities to the words found in Latin. If we look at early documents in Old English, around AD 800, we will find the word for 'father'. It's written 'feder' or 'fæder' (the <æ> was a way of writing an [a] sound). In Old High German it's 'fater'. In Old Frisian it's 'fadar' or 'feder'. The words have changed a bit today, but we can still see the similarities: modern English 'father', modern German 'Vater' (the word is spelled with a capital letter in German), modern Dutch 'vader'.

Obviously this is another family: the *Germanic* family of languages. And as we look around other parts of Europe, we'll find several other families. Welsh, Gaelic, Breton, and a few other languages form a *Celtic* family of languages. Russian, Polish,

Czech, and several others form a *Slavic* family. And there are some languages which, as it were, never had children. Greek stands all alone, as do the languages of Armenia and Albania.

For a long time, linguists studied languages by looking at small groups in this way. Then in 1785, Sir William Jones, a judge working in India, made a remarkable suggestion. He was a true multilingual, familiar with over 40 languages, speaking several of them fluently. But he didn't just speak them; he also thought about them. And he noticed the similarities between them. Eventually he proposed that actually many of these languages might belong to the same family – even though they were spoken by people living thousands of miles apart from each other.

He looked at the languages of India, especially one called Sanskrit. He looked at Greek and Latin. He looked at Persian, the Celtic languages, and others. And he concluded that the similarities were so great that they couldn't possibly have been produced by accident. Surely, he said, they all come from an ancient parent language, which perhaps no longer exists?

He was right. This ancient language we now call *Indo-European*. Nobody knows exactly where the Indo-European people lived. Some think it was in the steppe lands of southern Russia; some think it was further south, nearer to Turkey; and various other locations have been suggested. Nor is anybody certain about when exactly the Indo-Europeans were on the move. It might have been around 3000 BC, but could have been a lot earlier. Still, wherever and whenever they started, they eventually travelled east into India and west into Europe. And their language changed dramatically along the way.

Whatever the Indo-European word for 'father' was, it's clear that one group of people ended up in Italy, where the language became Latin, and the word for 'father' became 'pater'. Another group ended up in Scandinavia, where the language became Germanic, and the word for 'father' became 'fater'. Another group ended up in India, where the word for father (in Sanskrit) became 'piter'. Another group ended up in Ireland, where the word for father became 'athir'. By comparing all these, linguists have worked out

that the original word was probably something like *pəter. The [ə]
is a special symbol representing a sound like the 'e' of 'the'. And the
asterisk is there to show that we're guessing!

We have to do a lot of guessing when we look at the languages
of the world. Did all the aboriginal languages of Australia come

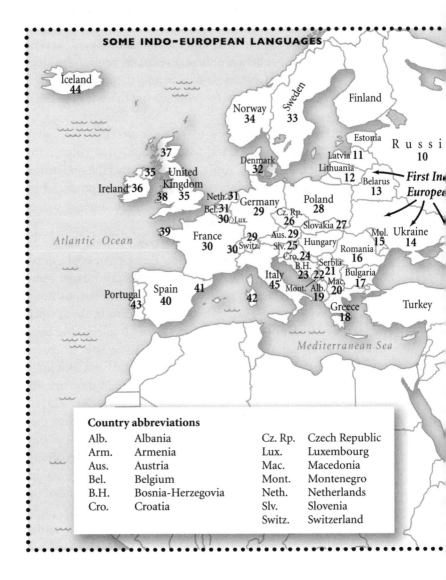

SOME INDO-EUROPEAN LANGUAGES

Iceland 44

Norway 34

Sweden 33

Finland

Estonia

Russi 10

Latvia 11

Lithuania 12

Belarus 13

First In Europe

United Kingdom 35 37 38 35

Ireland 36

Denmark 32

Neth. 31

Germany 29

Poland 28

Cz. Rp. 26

Slovakia 27

Mol. 15

Ukraine 14

Atlantic Ocean

Bel. 31 30 Lux.

France 30 29 30 Switz.

Aus. 29

Slv. 25 Hungary

Romania 16

Cro. 24

B.H. 23

Serbia 22 21

Bulgaria 17

Italy 45

Mont. Alb. 20 19

Mac.

Greece 18

Turkey

Portugal 43

Spain 40 41

42

Mediterranean Sea

Country abbreviations

Alb.	Albania	Cz. Rp.	Czech Republic
Arm.	Armenia	Lux.	Luxembourg
Aus.	Austria	Mac.	Macedonia
Bel.	Belgium	Mont.	Montenegro
B.H.	Bosnia-Herzegovia	Neth.	Netherlands
Cro.	Croatia	Slv.	Slovenia
		Switz.	Switzerland

from a single source? Did all the languages of North America? There are 2,000 languages in Africa. They couldn't possibly have all come from a single original language – or could they? These are fascinating questions. And of course they lead to the most fascinating question of all: could all languages have come from just one original language?

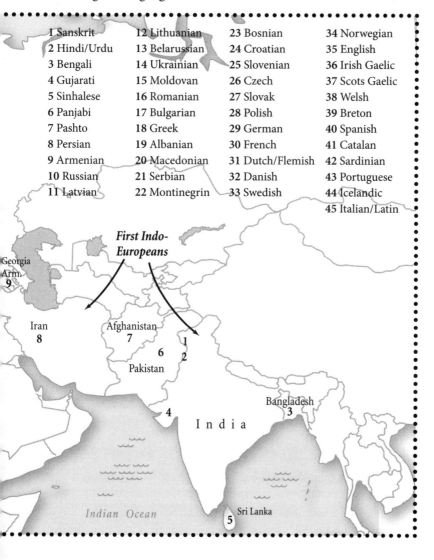

1 Sanskrit
2 Hindi/Urdu
3 Bengali
4 Gujarati
5 Sinhalese
6 Panjabi
7 Pashto
8 Persian
9 Armenian
10 Russian
11 Latvian

12 Lithuanian
13 Belarussian
14 Ukrainian
15 Moldovan
16 Romanian
17 Bulgarian
18 Greek
19 Albanian
20 Macedonian
21 Serbian
22 Montinegrin

23 Bosnian
24 Croatian
25 Slovenian
26 Czech
27 Slovak
28 Polish
29 German
30 French
31 Dutch/Flemish
32 Danish
33 Swedish

34 Norwegian
35 English
36 Irish Gaelic
37 Scots Gaelic
38 Welsh
39 Breton
40 Spanish
41 Catalan
42 Sardinian
43 Portuguese
44 Icelandic
45 Italian/Latin

First Indo-Europeans

Georgia
Arm.
9

Iran
8

Afghanistan
7

1
6 2

Pakistan

Bangladesh
3

I n d i a

4

Sri Lanka
5

Indian Ocean

CHAPTER 15

The origins of speech

When we go looking for language families, we find several parts of the world – such as Europe – where the evidence is clear-cut. The facts of history and of language reinforce each other, and we can say for certain that a family of languages exists. But this doesn't mean that every language in Europe belongs to the Indo-European family.

In northern Spain, and over the Pyrenees into south-west France, there's a language called Basque. It's totally unlike the other languages of Spain or indeed any of the other languages of Europe. It is an *isolated* language. It certainly doesn't belong to the Indo-European family. Its grammar is too different, and most of its words look as if they come from a different planet. Here's how you would say 'The woman has seen the man' in Basque:

emakumeak gizona ikusi du

It literally means:

woman-the man-the seen has

How did such a language come to be in the north of Spain?

Basque must be the last surviving language from the time *before* the Indo-Europeans arrived in the area. It's so long ago that we can't be sure who first lived in this part of Europe, or what languages were spoken. They would have been hunter-gatherers, wandering around Europe foraging for edible plants and animals. But they left no evidence of their language, because this was at a time before the human race learned to write (as we'll see in a later chapter).

If we try to compare Basque with the other languages of Europe, as we did when we were grouping the Romance and Germanic languages together in Chapter 14, we won't get very far. We'd find many words which the Basque people have borrowed from their neighbours over the centuries, such as 'eliza', the word for 'church', which clearly comes from Latin 'ecclesia'. But these wouldn't be enough to make us think that the languages had a common origin. Most Basque words are nothing like Latin or Romance words. So we would conclude, rightly, that Basque is isolated.

When we look at the languages of the world, we find hundreds of isolated languages. And there are hundreds more where the relationship between the different languages is very uncertain indeed. The Japanese and Korean languages have enough similarities for some people to think that they're related, but the differences are also very great, so the issue is controversial. Indeed, when we look at all the language families of the world, the differences between them stand out much more than the similarities. There seems very little in common between Indo-European languages and, for example, the languages of China or the aboriginal languages of Australia. Could they all have come from a single source? It's possible. But it's also possible that, when the human race first learned to talk, it did so in different parts of the world in different ways, and perhaps even at different times.

When did speech begin? Before creatures can speak, two things have to be in place. They need a set of vocal organs that can make all the sounds they will use to form lots of different words. And they need a brain that can handle all these sounds, and turn them into meaningful words and sentences. Our nearest relatives in the animal kingdom, such as the apes, can't talk. So when, in the long course of evolution from ape to man, did it happen?

The human-like beings that were living in Europe between 100,000 and 30,000 BC could have had some kind of primitive speech. Many skeletons have been found, and researchers have made plaster casts of the bony cavities inside their skulls, showing that their brain sizes were similar to those found in modern humans. None of the actual brains survive, of course, so it's not possible to say any more than that. But it's an important clue.

What about their vocal organs? Here too we don't have very much information, because a skeleton only gives us bones. We can see the shape of the jaws and the bony structures surrounding the mouth and in the neck; but all the soft tissues that made up the tongue and the larynx have long disappeared. Still, researchers have compared the shape of the skull and neck bones with those of modern human babies and adults, and worked out that these beings might have been able to produce a few speech-like sounds. The sounds wouldn't have been as many or as organized as those we find in modern languages; but these beings would certainly have been able to make far more sounds than apes can do. So probably, by 30,000 BC, they were well on the way to speaking, and perhaps had a few simple words expressing basic human emotions and needs, such as shouts of warning.

They would probably have had some sign language too. They were no longer walking around with their knuckles on the ground, as the apes did. Their hands were now free to do all kinds of exciting new things, such as make tools, or draw pictures inside their caves. They soon have learned to use their hands to make gestures, such as 'come here' or 'keep away'. And if they made sounds at the same time as they were making these gestures, maybe after a while these sounds would do the job that the gestures did, in places where the gestures couldn't be seen (such as in the dark and around corners).

As we'll see in the next chapter, by 8000 BC there is clear evidence of language ability in humans from the first signs of writing in various parts of the world. So, around 100,000 BC, maybe a bit earlier, and certainly well before 8000 BC, people began to talk. That's actually quite a short period of time, when we think of the hundreds of thousands of years that it took the human race to evolve from its earliest forms. Speaking seems to have been one of the last things to develop. But once it did, everyone must have seen its value very quickly.

Think of all the things you can do, once you can speak, that you couldn't do before. You can tell other people about dangers that they can't see. If there's a dangerous animal hiding in some rocks a mile away, you can warn others about it before they get there. Without speech, all you can do is point and howl, and that's not very clear if others can't see what you're pointing at. And if you spend a lifetime learning about all kinds of useful things, such as making tools, it's much easier to pass this knowledge on to your children if you can speak.

And think about how much easier it is to fight an enemy if you can talk. You can plan your strategy in advance. 'We'll wait until the sun goes down. Then you two go behind the trees, and wait there until I call ... We'll go round behind the rock at the bottom of the hill ... ' Without that, everyone just goes down the hill and hopes for the best.

It's easy to see, then, how speech would soon catch on, once early humans began to experiment with it. We don't know if the ability to talk started in just one small community, and spread to others, or whether different communities learned how to talk at more or less the same time – or even at different times. What we do know is that, within a few thousand years, different language families had emerged. The evidence is that some of them were beginning to be written down.

THE SPEAKING ANIMAL

Human beings have sometimes been called the 'speaking animal'. And because language is so important to them, it plays a large part in the myths, legends, and religious beliefs of people all over the world. Most cultures have stories of how language began.

Usually it's a god or gods who taught humans to speak or write. In one legend of the Chinese people, a water-turtle comes down from heaven with marks on its back, and these show people how to write. The people of Ancient Egypt believed that one of their gods, Thoth, was the scribe for the other gods, writing down their laws, and it was he who taught the skill of writing to the Egyptians. In the Bible, one of the first things Adam has to do, after being created, is name all the animals.

Some people have been so curious about how language began that they've actually carried out an experiment using babies. One famous story dates from the seventh century BC, and is about an Egyptian king, Psamtik I. He wanted to find out which of the peoples of the world was the most ancient, and he thought that if he could discover the world's first language, this would be the evidence he needed.

He knew that babies learn the speech of those around them. So, he figured, if two newborn babies were brought up in a situation where they heard no speech at all, when the time came for them to want to talk to each other, out would pop the world's original language from deep within their brains.

So he put two newborns into the care of a shepherd. He was to feed them goat's milk and generally look after them, but on no account was he ever to say anything within their hearing. Nor were they ever to hear anyone else talking. When they came out with their first words, he was to tell Psamtik immediately what they were.

The story goes that one day, when the children were about two, the shepherd went into the room where the children were, and they rushed to him holding out their hands and calling 'becos, becos'. He told the king, who then asked his advisers what language it was. 'It's the word for "bread" in the Phrygian language', they said. This disappointed Psamtik, who had hoped that the children would come out with an Egyptian word. But he had to accept the result of the experiment.

Of course – if it ever really happened – the whole thing was crazy. If children don't hear any language, they won't learn to talk. And Phrygian certainly wasn't any older than other languages spoken at the time. (It's a dead language now, but in Psamtik's day it was spoken in a part of the country we now call Turkey.)

So why did the children say 'becos'? Probably what the shepherd heard was the way the children had come to string together some of their sounds they babbled to each other. Maybe they'd come to associate these sounds with the idea of 'food'. Or maybe, quite simply, they were imitating the sound of the sheep or the goats!

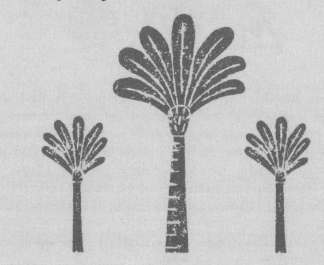

The origins of writing

Here are some road traffic signs.

You'll see Numbers 1–5 on roads in Europe; 6–7 in the USA. Number 1 means that there's a roundabout ahead. Number 2 means pedestrians could be crossing the road. Number 3 means that the speed limit is 60. Number 4 means that here is a place to park. Number 5 means that a double bend is coming up. Number 6 tells us which main road we are on. And the meaning of number 7 should be obvious. We have to learn signs like these when we learn to drive.

All seven signs are giving us information in the same sort of way. But which of them can we call 'writing'?

Numbers 6 and 7 contain words, so they are clearly writing. And most people would say that 3 and 4 are examples of writing too, because we have to read numerals '6' and '0' and the letter 'P'. The others look more like drawing. But that's only because we know there aren't letters in English which look like the signs in 1, 2, and 5.

Imagine being an alien from another galaxy. How would it know that the sign in number 4 was a letter and the sign in number 5 wasn't? Number 5 could easily be a letter: it actually looks like a backwards 'N' or an 'S' on its side. And number 1 is just like an 'O', except that there are three spaces in it.

It's no good telling the alien that numbers 1, 2, and 5 are pictures of the real world. All it would do is go and look at an actual roundabout and say (if it could talk): 'I can't see any spaces like it shows in the sign. Nor does the road bend coming up look exactly like that. And none of you people look like the thing in the sign. Half of you are wearing skirts, for a start, and the person in the sign isn't. Does that mean that you don't have to take care when people in skirts are crossing the road?'

Of course, we know what's happened. The people who have designed the signs have deliberately made things simple. As long as the signs remind us of a real roundabout, and a real person (male or female), and real road bends, they'll do. They're not supposed to be accurate.

Now imagine being one of the archaeologists digging in the deserts of the Middle East to find ancient remains. Our spade hits a hard object. It turns out to be a piece of stone, and on it is a circle with a dot inside it. Is this writing or not? Is it a letter of some unknown alphabet? Or is it a drawing of the sun, or a wheel, or something else? Often we can't be sure.

Deciding when human beings first started to write is quite tricky, because it's a problem deciding whether the marks they made are drawings or part of a writing system. A drawing of a buffalo on the wall of a cave is definitely art, not writing. The marks only look like writing when they start being used to replace drawings, have a definite size and shape, and appear on a surface in a line with a particular direction. The day I kill three buffaloes and draw them as three dead animals on my cave wall, I'm being an artist. But the day I kill three buffaloes and invent a sign for them (such as ^=^) and mark up on my cave-wall '^=^ 1 1 1', then I'm being a writer.

We see signs of this kind of system emerging from around 30,000 BC. People started to cut marks in sticks or on bones to show numbers of things. They're called 'tally-sticks' and 'tally-bones'. We don't know what they were counting. A stick with five cuts in it might have meant five animals or five units of grain, or five – anything.

The next step was to distinguish types of things, using clay. This happened around 9000 BC. Small lumps of clay were shaped into a ball, or a cone, or a rectangle, and so on. They're called *clay tokens*, because they were used to stand for things. A ball might mean a sheep; five balls would then mean five sheep. A cone might mean a cow; three cones would mean three cows. Again, we don't know what they were counting. However, we can guess, because this was the period when people were beginning to set up farms, so it would have been important to keep track of the number of animals someone had or the amount of grain they were selling.

Around 4000 BC there was another development. People started making marks on the clay tokens to show different types of things. One type of mark (such as X) might mean a male pig; another type of mark (such as O) might mean a female pig. So if I sent my servant to my cousin in another village with five pigs, and three of my pig-tokens had Xs on them and two had Os on them, everyone there would know what I was sending.

But there was a problem. What if my servant wasn't honest? Say I gave him these five pig-tokens, but when he got to my cousin's farm he showed him only four? He'd stopped off on the way and hidden one of the pigs for himself, and destroyed one of the tokens to hide what he'd done. My cousin wouldn't know any better. Four pigs – four tokens. No problem. No phones around in those days to check.

We can imagine that it didn't take long before people realized that this sort of thing was going on. And they hit on a clever solution. They bored holes in the tokens, and strung them together like a necklace. Then they joined the ends of the necklace together with another piece of clay and made their own personal mark (their *seal*) on it. I might choose +++ as my seal, for instance. Now the servant can't steal anything. If he broke the seal, he'd be found out.

Another clever way was to put all your tokens into a hollow clay ball, then seal the entrance hole with another piece of clay, and put your seal on that. It was a really safe method. No servant could get at the tokens without breaking the container – and then they'd be found out straight away.

But it can't have been long before someone noticed a problem with this way of doing things. What if someone stops my servant on the way and asks 'What are you carrying there?' The servant might not know. And there was no way of seeing inside. So people hit on the idea of showing the tokens on the outside of the container. The clay was quite soft, so all they had to do was take each token and press it down into the clay so that you could see its shape. Now anyone who wanted to know what was in the container would simply have to look at the marks on the outside – just as, today, a label on a bottle tells us what its contents are.

'But what's the point of that?' you might say. If there are now marks on the outside of the clay to show what the tokens are, then why did they need to have the tokens inside as well? Why not just let the marks do the job? Why not get rid of the tokens altogether and just put the marks representing sheep, pigs, and everything else onto a clay tablet? That would be a lot simpler.

And that's exactly what they did. By around 3400 BC, a writing system had begun to develop in which scribes scratched marks into clay tablets. A thousand years later, these had become clusters of small straight wedge-shaped marks, made by the end of a reed. The system was called *cuneiform* (pronounced 'kyoo-ni-form') – a name that comes from *cuneus*, the Latin word for 'wedge'.

The earliest cuneiform writing has been found in the ruins of the ancient city of Uruk, on the banks of the River Euphrates in modern Iraq. It had about 800 signs, representing numbers, types of produce (such as 'sheep' and 'fish'), and parts of the body (such as 'head' and 'mouth'), as well as everyday objects (such as 'pot' and 'plough'). Many of the signs were pictorial – for instance, the sign for a head actually looked like a head. ♪ But over the centuries, the writers picked out only the main features – just like a modern traffic sign. They also turned the picture on its side, to make it easier to write. The result looked like this: ⊨⊣ If you look at it sideways, you can just about see the resemblance to a head.

Eventually cuneiform writing came to be used for all kinds of purposes, such as making lists of possessions, sending messages between governments, and recording events. It was easy to see the value of a writing system of this kind, and soon other languages in the region started to use it. In fact it lasted for over 2,000 years, and only died out when more convenient ways of writing were invented, as we'll see in the next chapter.

Cuneiform was, as far as we know, the world's first true writing system. The Egyptians had a writing system too, of a rather different kind, but that started later. And the kinds of writing that developed elsewhere, such as in China or among the Mayas of Central America, were also much later. Early Chinese writing is found from around 1200 BC and Mayan writing from around 500 BC. The systems aren't related in any way. Humans invented writing several times over, in different parts of the world.

CHINESE WRITING

Read this sentence aloud: $3 + $6 = $9. It consists of a series of individual signs – $, +, =, 3, 6, 9 – which we learn to read as whole words. We could of course write them out in letters, like this:

> three dollars plus six dollars equals nine dollars

But that would waste an awful lot of time.

Signs like this are called *logographs*. The 'logo' part comes from a Greek word meaning 'word'. Logographs are 'word-signs'.

English doesn't have many logographs. Here are a few more:

& % @ £

We would read those as 'and', 'per cent', 'at', and 'pound'. And in maths we have several more, such as the signs for 'minus', 'multiplied by', 'divided by', and 'square root of'. Quite a few of the special signs in chemistry and physics are logographs, too.

Some languages consist entirely of logographs. Chinese is the best known. It's possible to write Chinese with an alphabet like the one we use for English, but the traditional way of writing the language is to use logographs – though they're usually called *characters* when we talk about Chinese. Here are two:

house   person

In these signs, we can easily see the picture origins of the characters. The 'house' character looks like a house, and the 'person' character clearly has two legs. But you might have some difficulty working out what these are:

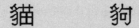

The first is 'cat' and the second is 'dog'. Most Chinese characters no longer closely resemble the way things look in the world. And of course there are thousands of meanings which don't have any shape at all, such as 'love' and 'see'. Here you don't get any help from the shape of the characters at all.

love   see

This system of writing is very different from the alphabetical way we're used to writing in English. That's the main reason English speakers think that Chinese is a difficult language to learn – but if we make the effort, it's really worth it.

CHAPTER 17

Modern writing

How could I write my name down in the languages of the world? One way would be to use the technique outlined in Chapter 16, and create a sign which meant 'David Crystal'. It might be ôô. But if everybody did that, it would soon be difficult to remember what such signs meant. We'd remember the signs for our relatives and friends, but imagine trying to find someone in a telephone directory, if everyone had their own personal sign!

It didn't take people long, in the history of writing, to realize that picture-writing, though simple to start with, has its limitations. It quickly becomes cumbersome. So they looked for ways of making it easier. One way was to add some signs which stood for the sounds of the language, and these were used along with the pictures to make new words. Here's how they did it.

You may have seen puzzles in books like this. First we see a picture and have to say it aloud:

'Bee'. Now we add letters to it, and have to say the new words aloud.

T

That would be 'beat'.

 F

That would be 'beef'. And so on. Once we've learned the sound of the picture, we can use it to help make up all kinds of new words – 'been', 'beak', 'beer', 'beads', and so on. If you've seen pictures of writing on the walls of Egyptian pyramids, the same sort of thing is going on – except they used their own signs to do it. They didn't have any letters like ours.

Once people got the idea that signs could stand for sounds, it wasn't long before they thought of writing *all* the sounds of a language down. Because languages have quite a small number of sounds, they realized that this would be a very good way of avoiding the problem of having to remember thousands of different signs. But there are two ways of writing down sounds.

Let's go back to my surname, 'Crystal', and think of it as a sequence of sounds, not letters. It has two 'beats', or 'pulses' of sound, which we can show like this:

Crys   tal

These beats form the rhythm of the word. They're called *syllables*. In a word like 'telephone' there are three syllables:

te – le – phone

In a word like 'supercalifragilisticexpialidocious' there are 14:

su per ca li fra gi li stic ex pi a li do cious

Some languages have developed writing systems where the signs stand for the different syllables. So there would be one sign for 'su', another for 'per', another for 'ca', and so on. A system which writes down syllables in this way is called a *syllabary*. There are several different ways of writing Japanese, for instance, and two of them are syllabaries. I'll explain how one of them works. It's called *katakana*.

The first thing we have to know is that Japanese pronunciation isn't like English. Syllables don't have the kind of Consonant + Vowel + Consonant pattern that we saw in English (at the end of Chapter 5). Japanese syllables usually have just two parts: Consonant + Vowel. They have syllables like 'wa', 'su', 'ke'.

Nor do the Japanese like to string consonants together – unlike English, which has words like 'street', where we hear three consonants at the front. Because of that, many Japanese people have difficulty pronouncing my surname, which has a [kr] at the beginning and a [st] in the middle. It's also got a [l] sound at the end. So they end up saying it like this:

C   ry s   ta l
ku ri su   ta ru

And if they wanted to write it in the katakana alphabet, they would put one sign for each syllable, and it would appear like this:

ku   ri   su   ta   ru

クリスタル

Not many languages have been written using a syllabary. Although it's a very clever way of writing, there are quite a large number of syllables in a language, so we have to learn a considerable number of signs. Katakana has 48. Some other syllabaries have several hundred. There has to be a simpler way.

And there is. It's called an *alphabet*. Let's think of my surname as a sequence of individual sounds, not syllables. It has seven sounds, and each one is shown by a single letter.

Crystal

This method of writing, where a letter stands for a sound, is called *alphabetic*. And the set of letters which the language uses is called its *alphabet*.

Examples of alphabetic writing date from around 1800 BC, in various parts of the Middle East – the earliest we know of was discovered in Egypt in the 1990s. The most influential alphabet, from around 1000 BC, is called the North Semitic alphabet, which was used in parts of Palestine and Syria. It had 22 letters, all consonants. The modern Hebrew and Arabic alphabets have come down from it. Later, the Greeks took this alphabet over and added extra marks for vowels. Later still, the Romans took over the Greek alphabet and made more changes. And the Roman alphabet is the one we use for writing English and many other languages today. It's the most widely used writing system in the world.

Why did the alphabet become so popular? Because it's a system which uses only a small number of units – just 26 for English. The language of the Rotokas people of Papua New Guinea has 12. Some languages have as many as 50 or so, but most have a much smaller number.

It's a great idea. Once we've learned our alphabet we can write down any word we like. We can even make up nonsense words and people will be able to read them. Doolaboola! We can read the names of people we've never heard of. If we got an email from a man called Alipo Matak, we'd have a good idea about how he pronounced his name.

Unfortunately, as we saw in Chapter 9, with some languages the alphabet idea doesn't work so well in practice. It works fine when each letter stands for just one sound. That's called writing *phonetically*, and some languages, such as Spanish and Welsh, are written in a very phonetic way – with only a few exceptions. Even English was phonetic, when the monks who came to Britain first wrote it down in Anglo-Saxon times.

It's the obvious way to start. If you had the task of writing down a language for the first time – and, as we'll see in a later chapter, many of the world's languages have never been written down – then you'd listen carefully to the individual sounds, and assign a different letter to each one.

The problem would come when you had to write down a language which had lots of sounds. You'd soon run out of letters! And this was the case with English. The monks tried to use the Latin alphabet they knew, which had 23 letters, to write English, and they quickly found that there were sounds in the new language which were nothing like the sounds of Latin. The two 'th' sounds – the ones we hear in *thin* and *this* – were new, so the monks looked for letters in a different alphabet to write them down. The runic alphabet was also being used in northern Europe at the time, and there they found þ and ð. We don't use those letters any more in writing English, but they exist in manuscripts throughout Anglo-Saxon times.

But even these extra letters weren't enough. English has actually got 44 different sounds, and with only 26 letters it's obvious that there's going to be a problem. One way of getting round the problem is to use double letters to show differences in sound. We can see how this works in spellings like this, which I've taken from some comics. How would you read these words aloud?

CRASH!   CRAASH!   CRAAASH!!!

The more A's there are, the longer you keep the sound going. And that's exactly how people do it, when they're writing a language down. Read these words aloud.

met   meet   lot   loot

The double letters show that the vowel is longer. And people thought up other ways of using two letters to show one sound, as we can see from such spellings of the long [ee] vowel as 'meat', 'Pete', and 'field', as well as such combinations as <sh> and <th> for single consonant sounds.

In these ways, English was written down, and for the first few hundred years of the language, the letters and sounds matched each other quite well. But gradually the way people pronounced English changed (as we saw in Chapter 9), and the letters ceased to reflect the sounds. That's why today one letter can stand for many sounds: <g>, for example, sounds differently in the words 'good', 'George', and 'genre', and isn't pronounced at all in such words as 'sign' and 'gnaw'. Also, one sound can be spelled with many letters. The same 'oo' sound of 'loot' is heard in 'dude', 'two', 'do', 'group', 'fruit', and 'grew', and has some really strange spellings in words from other languages, such as 'canoe', 'rheumatism', and 'manoeuvre'.

One of the big differences between English and languages such as French, German, or Spanish is that it never went in for accent marks. (This is a different sense of the word 'accent' from the one I used in Chapter 12.) We see <é>, <ê>, and <è> in French, for example, <ä>, <ü>, and <ö> in German, and <ñ> in Spanish. The accent changes the way the letter sounds.

When English borrowed accented words from these languages, it sometimes took the accents too, so we do see the occasional word spelled with an accent, especially if it's needed to tell words apart:

The rose was expensive (pronounced 'rohz') – a flower
The rosé was expensive (pronounced 'roh-zay') – a bottle of
  wine

Accents also remind us how to pronounce a word:

fiancé – pronounced 'fee-on-say'
naïve – pronounced 'ny-eeve'

But once a word becomes very well known, the accent is usually dropped. These days we see 'cafe', 'decor', 'discotheque', and 'seance' much more often than 'café', 'décor', 'discothèque' and 'séance'. Some people get very cross about this, and insist on putting the accents in. When you study modern writing systems, be prepared for varying usages – and differing opinions!

DELTA CHARLIE HERE

People often say that the alphabet is one of the world's greatest inventions, because – like the wheel – it allows us to do an amazing number of things. It doesn't just enable us to write. It helps us organize our lives.

Alphabetical order is the reason. We learn the alphabet in a fixed sequence – A, B, C, D … In English, the first letter is A, the last is Z. And that allows us to find our way around library shelves, telephone directories, website indexes, and all sorts of places where people have used letters to classify information.

Each letter has a name: in English, 'B' is pronounced 'bee'; 'M' is pronounced 'em'. But in a noisy situation, sometimes it's difficult to hear the names clearly. And if we spell out a word over the phone, the person at the other end often can't hear whether we're saying 'P' or 'B', or 'M' or 'N'.

For that reason, the police, army, and other organizations gave the letters 'bigger' names, which could be heard more clearly when people are talking by phone or radio. One of the most widely used was created by the group of countries that form NATO, the North Atlantic Treaty Organization. The *NATO phonetic alphabet*, as it's usually called, goes like this:

A	Alpha	B	Bravo	C	Charlie
D	Delta	E	Echo	F	Foxtrot
G	Golf	H	Hotel	I	India
J	Juliet	K	Kilo	L	Lima
M	Mike	N	November	O	Oscar
P	Papa	Q	Quebec	R	Romeo
S	Sierra	T	Tango	U	Uniform
V	Victor	W	Whiskey	X	X-ray
Y	Yankee	Z	Zulu		

You've probably heard it on TV. If you wanted to spell out my surname in this alphabet, you'd begin 'Charlie Romeo ...' I rather like that!

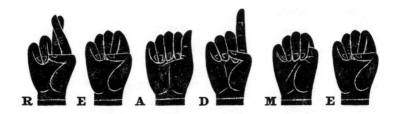

CHAPTER 18

Sign language

Speech and writing are two of the ways in which we encounter language. But there's a third way.

It's a common sight these days. We're watching a programme on TV, and in the corner of the screen is a box in which someone is gesturing, mouthing, and making lively facial expressions. What's going on?

The person is using *sign language*, for the benefit of any deaf people who may be watching. The signer is a hearing person who has learned a deaf sign language.

Which sign language signers use depends on which part of the world they're in. If they're working in the UK, they'll be presenting British Sign Language. If they're in France, it'll be French Sign Language. If they're in China, it'll be Chinese Sign Language. Around the world, different sign languages have evolved among deaf people over hundreds of years. Maybe much longer.

Nobody knows how long sign language has existed. An early form of signing was probably around when the human brain developed enough to make language possible. We saw in Chapter 15 that the beings who lived earlier than 30,000 years ago didn't have the physical ability to make many vocal sounds. But they could use their hands. Maybe they were able to use their hands to make signs.

It's a pretty natural thing to do, after all. We've all got a few hand signals that we can use to express some basic meanings. I can give you a thumbs up to show that everything's OK. I can wave to say hello or goodbye. I can shake my fist if I'm angry. But these are all very simple notions, and there aren't many gestures that we regularly use in this way. A couple of dozen, only. We can't say very much with that.

There are a few jobs where people have had to develop their signing a bit more fully. We see referees and umpires using their arms and hands to signal directions to the players – as in cricket, where a single finger upwards means that the batsman is out and has to leave the wicket. Orchestra conductors control the musicians through their movements. People working at a distance from each other have to invent special signals if they want to communicate. So do people working in a noisy environment, such as in a factory where the machines are very loud, or lifeguards around a swimming pool full of school children.

But the signing in these situations is there to solve a 'local' problem. The signs aren't much use in other places. It wouldn't be any good if I wanted someone to leave the room and I raised a single finger in the air. They wouldn't know what I was getting at. Nor would it be much use if I tried to get a group of friends to behave in a certain way by waving my arms about like the conductor of an orchestra. They'd probably lock me up if I started doing that.

So these kinds of signing aren't like real languages. Real languages have thousands of words which can be joined together to make thousands of sentences to talk about anything we want. The signs used by umpires and crane drivers are very limited in their range and meaning. It wouldn't be much use my asking a football referee or an orchestra conductor to use their signs to explain how a car engine works or to say what the latest bestselling pop song is.

That's the big difference with the sign languages used by deaf people. Deaf sign languages *are* used to express the same sort of complicated thoughts that hearing people want to express when they speak or write. Deaf sign languages have several thousand signs, which can be used in sequences to do the same job as the sentences of spoken and written language. And when we see signers on television, they're translating everything they hear into sign language – and working at great speed.

There are two really important things to remember about deaf sign languages. First, deaf people don't simply take the words from spoken language and translate them into signs. It's possible to invent a deaf sign language which follows the words of speech – and that's been done several times – but the kind of thing we see on television screens doesn't work like that. The signs directly express meanings – a bit like the way logographic signs do (as we saw with Chinese in Chapter 16).

So if a signer heard me say this sentence:

The boy who won the long jump has also won the high jump

we wouldn't see signs for 'the', then 'boy', then 'who', and so on. What we'd see is something like:

boy + win + past time + long jump + also + high jump

Nor would the signs need to come out in that particular order. Sometimes they would follow the word order of the English sentence, but sometimes they wouldn't. The usual way of signing 'What's your name?' in British Sign Language is:

your name + what

along with a puzzled facial expression, such as raised eyebrows.

The second thing to remember about deaf sign languages is that they're very different from each other. Just as we don't expect someone who speaks only English to understand Chinese, so we mustn't expect someone who knows only British Sign Language to understand Chinese Sign Language. Nor, surprising as it seems, does someone who knows only British Sign Language even understand American Sign Language. These two sign languages have gone in very different directions over the past 200 years. There are a few similar signs, but they aren't enough to make the languages intelligible to each other.

A few years ago, Mark Medoff wrote a play called *Children of a Lesser God* about the relationship between a deaf student and her hearing teacher, who falls in love with her. It was also made into a film starring William Hurt and Marlee Matlin. The play is set in the USA, so they communicate with each other using American Sign Language. But when the play came to London, British deaf people couldn't understand the signs, and they had to employ an interpreter to translate from American into British Sign Language.

You might think that at least some of the signs used by the deaf will be shared by all the sign languages of the world. What about the sign for 'elephant'? Surely that will always have a hand movement showing the distinctive trunk? But actually, there's more than one way in which we can show a trunk. Do we start at the nose and make a shape sideways or towards the front? Do we make a hand movement downwards or upwards? Is the hand movement straight or curved? Is the shape of the hand flat or in a 'C' shape? How fast do we make the sign? There are obviously many possibilities, even in the case of something as easy to see as an elephant. And when we start to think of such notions as 'garden', 'blue', or 'argue', it's clear that different sign languages will express them in many different ways.

All the important notions that we use in studying spoken and written language are needed in relation to sign language too. For instance, we'll find dialects and accents, just as we saw in Chapter 12. Deaf people from one part of a country will have a few signs that differ from those used in other places. And if someone from Britain went to China, and started to learn Chinese Sign Language, they would make the Chinese signs but probably not in exactly the Chinese way. For instance, the sign for 'father', which involves closing the fingers over the palm of the hand, might be made with fingers very straight and tense, as in the drawing on the left (see next page), or with the fingers slightly bent and relaxed, as on the right:

There are several other possibilities. A British person would be likely to make it with the fingers relaxed, and that would be noticed by a Chinese deaf person as a foreign accent.

It all adds up to one thing. Never think of deaf signing as if it were simply a set of primitive gestures. It's as complex and useful and beautiful as any spoken or written language.

FINGER-SPELLING

What about names? How would a deaf person sign 'David Crystal', or your name, or the town where you live? There won't be separate signs for these notions, because there are too many of them – hundreds of thousands of names of people and places.

The solution is to spell them out, using the fingers. Anyone can learn to finger-spell – but there are two systems, depending on whether we do it with one hand or two. It's quick to learn, and it can immediately be used to spell any word – not just names of people and places, but also unusual words, such as an abstruse term in chemistry.

It does slow you down a bit. It's difficult to spell out more than 300 letters in a minute (which would be about 60 words). And it's not much use for young children who haven't learned to spell yet! But it's so useful that deaf people can't do without it, and they learn to speed up by abbreviating some words – a bit like texters do.

The Greek word for 'finger' is 'dactulos', and the 'ology' ending means 'knowledge'. So the technical name for 'finger-spelling' is *dactylology* – pronounced 'dak-til-<u>ol</u>-o-gee'.

The British system of finger-spelling uses two hands; it's used in the UK, Ireland, Australia, New Zealand, and a few other countries. The American system uses one; it's chiefly used in the USA and Canada. (It doesn't matter which hand you use. That depends on whether you're left-handed or right-handed.)

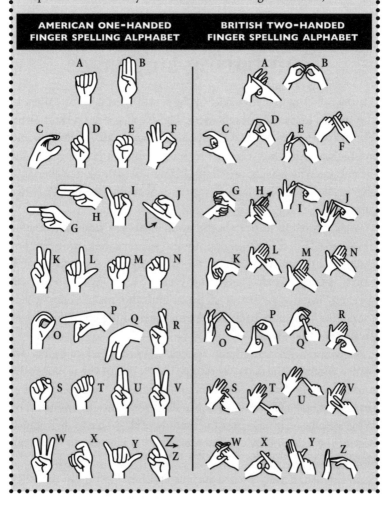

AMERICAN ONE-HANDED FINGER SPELLING ALPHABET

BRITISH TWO-HANDED FINGER SPELLING ALPHABET

CHAPTER 19

Comparing languages

All the 6,000 or so languages of the world have certain things in common. They've all got sentences. They've all got nouns and verbs. They've all got vowels and consonants. They've all got rhythm and intonation. But when we start to learn a foreign language, it's the differences which cause problems. It's natural to think that everyone else speaks their language in the same way that we do. Then we discover the reality is very different.

We'll probably notice the unfamiliar sounds first, and maybe have some difficulty getting our mouth to make them properly. For instance, English doesn't have the [ch] sound that's used in such words as Gaelic 'loch' ('lake') and Welsh 'bach' ('little'), so English speakers usually substitute a [k] sound and make these words sound like 'lock' and 'back'. But it only takes a little bit of practice to pronounce them well.

However, with some languages, it can take a while before we realize what the speakers are doing. This is one of the reasons why mother-tongue English speakers find Chinese a tricky language at first. Speakers of Chinese speak in a 'sing-song' way, to English ears. Why? Because Chinese uses the melody of the voice to distinguish between words, and this isn't something that happens in European languages.

In English, if I say a word such as 'mother' high up in my voice or low down in my voice, it makes no difference to the meaning of the word. It's still 'mother'. But in Chinese – and also in many other languages spoken in the Far East – that difference in pitch height can change the meaning of the word completely. The word 'ma', said high up in the voice and on a level note, means 'mother'. But if you say 'ma' low in the voice with a dip downwards followed by a rise in pitch, it means 'horse'. These differences in melody are called 'tones'. Chinese, we say, is a 'tone language'. It's very important to get the tones right, otherwise we'll end up calling our mother a horse!

The other thing we notice very quickly, when we begin to learn a language, is the unfamiliar grammar. Sometimes it's the order of words in a sentence which is different. In English we would say:

Sian is in the kitchen.

In Welsh we would say:

Mae Sian yn y gegin. (pronounced 'my shahn uhn uh geg-in')

If we translate this word by word, it comes out like this:

Mae Sian yn y   gegin.
Is   Sian in the kitchen.

When making a statement, Welsh puts the verb at the beginning of a sentence. English puts it in the middle. Some languages, such as Hindi, put it at the end.

Another example. In some languages, adjectives go before the noun; in others, they go after. English and German are two languages that put most of their adjectives before the noun:

a black cat
ein schwarze Katze (pronounced 'shvahrtsuh katsuh')

French (and also Welsh) puts most adjectives after the noun:

un chat noir (pronounced 'uhn sha nwahr')
a cat black

One of the biggest differences in grammar that English speakers
notice is if the new language signals meanings by changing the
endings of its words. This happens in only a few circumstances in
English – such as these:

- We can change most nouns from singular to plural by
  adding an 's': 'dog' becomes 'dogs'.
- We can change the time reference of most verbs from present
  to past by adding an 'ed': 'I walk' becomes 'I walked'.
- We can compare many adjectives by adding 'er' or 'est':
  'small' – 'smaller' – 'smallest'.

There are just a handful of other endings.

It comes as a bit of a surprise, then, when we find languages which
have dozens or even hundreds of word endings. Latin, spoken by
the Ancient Romans, is an example. It had sentences like this:

canis   vidit   puerum
the dog saw   the boys

and

puer   vidit   canem
the boy saw   the dog

When the dog is doing the seeing, the Latin word has a different
ending from when it is being seen – 'canis' instead of 'canem'. And
when the boy is doing the seeing, the Latin word has a different
ending from when they are being seen – 'puer' instead of 'puerum'.
These endings are called *cases*, and in Latin the case of a noun
changes depending on how it's being used in a sentence. There's
no quick way of learning cases. You just have to learn them off by
heart.

With a language like Latin, we know 'who's doing what' by paying attention to those word endings. The order of words in the sentence isn't important. That makes Latin a very different kind of language from English, where the order of words is crucial. In English, the noun that's doing the action comes first in the sentence; the noun that's receiving the action comes last. So these two sentences mean very different things:

the dog saw the boy
the boy saw the dog

But in Latin we can put the words in any order we like, because the meaning of 'who's doing what' is being signalled by the endings. So these two sentences mean the same thing:

puer vidit canem
canem vidit puer

In both cases, it's the boy who's doing the seeing and the dog which is being seen.

It usually takes a bit longer to notice differences in vocabulary. This is because, at first hearing, most words seem to work in the same way as English. The word for 'table' in Spanish is 'mesa'. In German it is 'Tisch'. It all seems very straightforward. Take a word and translate it into another language, and all will be well.

But quite soon we'll notice that it isn't as easy as that. Some words try to fool us. When we learn French we will meet the word 'demander'. This looks just like the English word 'demand', so naturally we think that's what it means. In fact it doesn't. It means 'ask'.

Words like 'demander' are called 'false friends'. On the surface they seem nice and familiar; but when we go beneath the surface it turns out that we don't know them at all. All languages give us some false friends. Walk around a town in Italy and sooner or later you'll see a place called a 'libreria'. Is it a library? No, it's a bookshop. The word for 'library' is quite different: 'biblioteca'.

We also find that some words don't match up in an easy one-to-one sort of way. Sometimes an English word can be translated by two or more different words in the foreign language. The word 'know', for example, can be translated as either 'savoir' or 'connaître' in French. If we know a fact or know how to do something, we have to use a form of 'savoir'. If we know a person, we have to use a form of 'connaître'. We can't say in French:

> je sais Marie (pronounced 'zhuh <u>say</u> Marie')
> I know Marie

It has to be:

> je connais Marie (pronounced 'zhuh ko<u>nay</u> Marie')
> I know Marie

Sometimes we find the opposite situation: a foreign word can be translated by two or more English words. Let's stay with French. Most English-speaking people know that 'je t'aime' means 'I love you' in French. But 'aime' can also mean 'like'. So we can say that we 'aime' chocolate or swimming or our cousin. How do French people tell the difference? If someone says they 'aime' you, are they liking you or loving you? It's usually obvious from the way other words are used in the sentence, or from the tone of voice – or, of course, from the associated actions. If a filmstar says 'Je t'aime' and gives someone a long passionate kiss, it doesn't just mean 'I like you'!

Conversations themselves can cause problems. In French the word for 'thank you' is 'merci' (pronounced 'mare-see'). So now, imagine you're in a cafe and someone asks you whether you want a cup of coffee. In English, the conversation might go like this:

> Do you want a coffee?
> Thank you.

And a few minutes later you'd have a coffee in front of you. But if you said this in French, the result would be very different:

Voulez-vous un café? (pronounced 'voolay vooz uhn kafay')
Merci.

No coffee would arrive. This is because 'merci' on its own like that means 'thanks but no thanks'. You're refusing. If you want to say 'yes', you would have to say 'yes' ('oui') or 'please' ('s'il vous plaît') or 'yes thanks' ('oui merci'), or the like.

We say 'please' a lot when we speak English. Our parents drum it into us from a very early age. In many other languages, it's not such an important word. We can be polite without saying their word for 'please'. In Spanish, for instance, the word for 'please' is 'por favor' (pronounced 'pawr favawr'), but you won't hear Spanish people saying it routinely in shops when they're asking for things. If you did hear someone say 'por favor', it would be because the speaker was feeling impatient or insistent – 'hurry up, if you please'!

There are lots of conversational differences like this. In English, we don't start saying 'good evening' until it's around 6 or 7 o'clock. In Italian they say the equivalent phrase ('buona sera', pronounced 'bwohna sayra') much earlier – from around 4 or 5 o'clock. In English, we don't say 'good morning' after 12 o'clock. In French, they say 'bonjour' (pronounced 'bonzhoor') for 'good morning' and carry on saying it in the afternoon as well. People have conversations in all languages, but never in exactly the same way.

HOW OLD ARE YOU?

In English, when we meet people for the first time, there are some topics which it's safe to talk about – such as the weather, or which part of the country they come from. We wouldn't ask them whether they were married, or how much they earned, or how old they were.

We learn these politeness rules very early on in life – from around age three. 'How old are you?' asks Auntie Ann at little Jimmy's fourth birthday party. 'I'm four', says Jimmy. And then he says, 'How old are you?' Everybody laughs. Jimmy is being very cute. But Auntie Ann won't say. And gradually, Jimmy learns that one thing you should never do is ask a lady her age!

It isn't just little Jimmy in the UK. This is one of the rules of polite conversation which is found in cultures and languages in many parts of the world. But not everywhere. In some Asian cultures questions about age or earnings are perfectly normal. It's just their way of being friendly.

CHAPTER 20

Dying languages

Speaking, writing, and signing are the three ways in which a language lives and breathes. They are the three mediums through which a language is passed on from one generation to the next. If a language is a healthy language, this is happening all the time. Parents pass their language on to their children, who pass it on to their children … and the language lives on.

Languages like English, Spanish, and Chinese are healthy languages. They exist in spoken, written, and signed forms, and they're used by hundreds of millions of people all over the world. But most of the 6,000 or so of the world's languages aren't in such a healthy state. They're used by very few people. The children aren't learning them from their parents. And as a result the languages are in real danger of dying out.

When does a language die?

A language dies when the last person who speaks it dies. And this is happening in many parts of the world. There are several dozen languages which have only one speaker left. And several more where the speakers are just a few dozen or fewer. For example, many of the languages spoken by the tribal peoples of Brazil or Indonesia have only a handful of speakers.

Languages which have only a few speakers, and which are likely to die out soon, are called *endangered* languages. Most of the world's endangered languages are spoken in countries on either side of the equator. There are hundreds of languages spoken in south-east Asia, in such countries as Papua New Guinea. Hundreds more are spoken across India and Africa. Many more are in South America. These are the places where languages are dying out very quickly.

But we can find endangered languages anywhere. Most of the Indian languages of North America are endangered. And so are the Celtic languages of Britain, Ireland, and France. Fewer and fewer people speak Gallic, the Celtic language of Scotland. And the last native speakers of Manx, the language of the Isle of Man, died out a few decades ago.

Perhaps half the languages of the world are going to die out in the next 100 years. That's 3,000 languages disappearing in 1,200 months. If we work out the average, we'll find that there's a language dying out somewhere in the world every two weeks or so. This is much faster than anything that's happened in the past.

There's nothing new about a language dying. Languages have always disappeared when the people who spoke them died out. Two thousand years ago there were many languages spoken throughout the Middle East that no longer exist today. Think of all the peoples who invented the writing systems that I described in Chapter 16, such as the Hittites, the Assyrians, and the Babylonians. Those cultures came and went, over thousands of years, as one defeated another, and the languages disappeared along with the peoples.

We know something about these ancient languages because some of them were written down. Unfortunately, many languages of the past were never written down, so they are lost for ever. That's still the case today. About 2,000 of the world's languages have never been written down. If they die before linguists get a chance to record them, they too will be gone for ever.

When a culture dies out, it leaves behind evidence of how the people lived. Archaeologists can dig up all sorts of things – pots, skeletons, boats, coins, weapons, bits of houses – but spoken language leaves nothing behind when it disappears. After all, as we saw in Chapter 4, speech is only vibrations in the air. So when a spoken language dies which has never been recorded in some way, it is as if it has never been.

There's nothing unusual about a single language dying. But what's going on today is extraordinary, when we compare the situation to what has happened in the past. We're seeing languages dying out on a massive scale. It's a bit like what's happening to some species of plants and animals. They're dying out faster than ever before. Why is this?

Plants and animals die out for all sorts of reasons, such as changes in climate, the impact of new diseases, or changes in the way people use the land. And some of these reasons apply to languages too. A natural disaster, such as an earthquake or a tsunami, can destroy towns and villages, and kill many people. But if the people are dead, or if their community is devastated, then their language will die out too.

Humans can be the cause of language death. Hunters can kill all the remaining animals in a species. Collectors can take all the remaining plants. And governments can stop people using their language – as we saw in Chapter 13. If a language is banned, and the children are forbidden to learn it, it will soon die out.

But the main reason that so many languages are endangered is not as sudden or as dramatic as a tsunami or a banning. In most cases, the people stop using their first language simply because they decide to use a different one. This is why, for example, most people in Wales speak English or most people in Brittany speak French. Over the years, families have gradually stopped using one language and started using another.

Why have they done this? It's usually because the new language promises them a better kind of life. In particular, they'll get a better job if they learn the new language. Think of all the 'best jobs' in the country where you live. How many of them would you be able to do if you didn't speak the main language of the country? None of them.

Now imagine being a member of a small tribe in Africa, America, or Australia a few hundred years ago, when the British, Spanish, and others were colonizing the world. In come the colonists with their guns and new ways of life, and they take over your country. They're in charge, so if you want to get on, in the new society, you've just got to learn their language. And when that happens, it's very easy to let your old language slip away. Your children don't bother with it, because the new language is the really useful one. It's fashionable. It's cool. Your old language is definitely uncool. And gradually, it falls out of use.

It doesn't have to be that way. People can learn a new language without having to lose their old one. That's what bilingualism is all about, as we saw in Chapter 13. Bilingualism lets you have your cake and eat it. The new language opens the doors to the best jobs in society; the old language allows you to keep your sense of 'who you are'. It preserves your identity. With two languages, you have the best of both worlds.

These days, in many countries, people have come to realize this. They see the importance of preserving the language diversity of the world, just as they see the importance of preserving the diversity of plants and animals. The world governing bodies, such as the United Nations, have repeatedly drawn attention to the issue. It isn't enough just to preserve the 'tangible' heritage of the Earth – all the physical things we can see around us in the landscape, such as deserts, forests, lakes, monuments, and buildings. It's also important to preserve the 'intangible' heritage – all the things which show how we live, such as music, dance, theatre, painting, crafts, and especially languages.

How do we preserve languages? Three factors have to be present for this to happen. The people themselves must want their language to survive. The government of their country must want to help them. And money has to be found to keep the language going. It's an expensive business. The language has to be documented – that is, written down and described in grammars and dictionaries. Teachers have to be trained, books published, street signs put up, community centres established, and lots more.

But when all three factors are in place, amazing things can be done. New life can be brought into a language. The term is *revitalization*. The language is *revitalized*. We've seen it happen several times over the past 50 years. Probably the most famous case is the revival of Hebrew to serve as the official language of modern Israel. Welsh, too, has done very well, after a long period of decline. Today the number of speakers is increasing, and its presence can be seen on street signs and in railway stations and wherever you travel in Wales.

In New Zealand, the Maori language has been kept alive by a system of 'language nests'. These are organizations that provide children under five with a homely setting in which they are intensively exposed to the language. The staff are all Maori speakers from the local community. The hope is that the children will keep their Maori skills alive after leaving the nests, and that as they grow older they will in turn help new generations of young children to learn the language.

Even an extinct language can be brought back to life, if conditions are right. It must have been written down and described, or audio-recorded in some way, and the people must want it back. This has happened with an Aboriginal language of South Australia called Kaurna. The last native speaker died in 1929, but in the 1980s a group of Kaurna people decided that they wanted their language back. 'The language isn't dead,' they said, 'it's only sleeping.' Fortunately, material survived from the nineteenth century so that a linguist was able to make a fresh description and help the Kaurna people start learning the language again. It's taught in schools now. One day, perhaps, some children will start learning it as their mother tongue.

One of the jobs the linguist had to do was bring the vocabulary up to date. The old Kaurna language had no words for television or mobile phones! That's the thing about a language: it never stands still. When we study language, one of the most important topics is to investigate the way languages change.

PARROT TALK

In 1801, an explorer called Alexander von Humboldt was searching for the source of the Orinoco river in South America. He met some Carib Indians who had recently attacked a neighbouring tribe. They'd killed all the people, but they'd brought the tribe's parrots back home with them.

The parrots chattered away, like parrots do. And when von Humboldt heard them talk, he realized that they were speaking the language of the murdered Indians. He decided to write the words down, to capture the sound of the language. There were no human speakers of the language left. The parrots were all he had to go on.

Nearly 200 years later, an American sculptor called Rachel Berwick decided to make the language come alive again. She got two South American parrots and taught them to say some of the words that von Humboldt had written down. Then she put them in a large cage surrounded by foliage and jungle noises, and displayed them in a gallery. The parrots happily chattered away.

Suddenly, the old language came alive again. Even though it was only parrot-talk, hearing it sent shivers down the back of your neck.

CHAPTER 21

Language change

All living languages change. They have to. Languages have no existence apart from the people who use them. And because people are changing all the time, their language changes too, to keep up with them. The only languages that don't change are dead ones. Even so, as we saw in Chapter 20, it's possible to bring a language back from the grave and make it live – and change – again.

Why does a language change? Sometimes the reason is obvious. If we invent something, we need a name for it, and at that point a new word comes into a language. Think of some of the words that have become widely used in English to talk about new developments during the early years of this century. Many of them are to do with the internet:

Google, blogging, texting, SMS, iPhone, instant message, Facebook, Twitter.

If we could time-travel back to 1990, and talk to the people, we'd have to make sure we didn't use any of these words, as they wouldn't know what we were talking about. Dr Who must have this problem all the time!

We'd notice something else, as we travelled back in time. The people wouldn't understand all our words; but sometimes we wouldn't understand theirs. Imagine our time machine arriving in, say, 1850. We'd hear conversations like this:

> We're coming in our brougham. The Smiths will be in their clarence. And the Browns will probably come in a landau.

What are broughams (pronounced 'brooms') and clarences and landaus? Types of horse-drawn four-wheeled carriages, popular in the second half of the nineteenth century. People stopped using them when motor cars were invented – though we'll sometimes see one on special occasions, such as when the Queen of England visits Ascot races.

New words come into use. Old words go out of use. This is a pattern we see in every area of human knowledge and every part of society. The old words never disappear entirely, of course. We see them every time we read an old book, and hear them whenever we go to see a play written a long time ago. Several people in Shakespeare's plays are called 'arrant knaves'. We'd say something like 'complete villains' in modern English. People stopped saying 'arrant knaves' around 300 years ago. But these words are still there in the plays, waiting for the actors to breathe new life into them.

Vocabulary is the area where we most often notice the way language changes, because each year hundreds of new words arrive in a language. We only come across a few of them in everyday life, of course. Most new words are technical terms to do with specialized areas of knowledge we don't know anything about, or they're slang words which are used by a very small group of people.

But every year we find ourselves using a few words and phrases that we never used before. Hardly anyone had met the term 'credit crunch' before 2008. Then suddenly everyone was using it. Each year the dictionary-writers publish lists of the latest words to come into the English language. Over the past few years they include 'sudoku', 'bling', 'plasma screen', and 'blog'. I wish I could say what new words are going to come into English in 2010. Unfortunately, I'm writing this book in 2009 and I can't see into the future. But by the time you get to read it, you'll know.

Every part of language changes. It's not just the words. Grammar changes. Pronunciation changes. The way we talk to each other changes. Even spelling and punctuation change. But not everything changes at the same rate.

When a new word comes into a language, it can be picked up and used by everyone within a few days. If it starts being used on the internet, millions of people can be using it within a few hours. Changes in the other areas of language take much longer. It might take 100 years or more before a change in grammar comes to be used by everyone.

Let's go back again in time to the nineteenth century. The novelist Jane Austen was writing in the early 1800s. Here's a sentence taken from one of her letters:

Jenny and James are walked to Charmouth this afternoon.

We couldn't say that today. These days we'd have to say:

Jenny and James walked to Charmouth this afternoon.

Nobody can say for sure when the 'are walked' way of talking stopped being used and the other way took over. We see it being used less and less during the nineteenth century, and then it just disappears.

Over the past 200 years lots of small changes like this have taken place in the way we construct sentences. Here are two more examples of old usages from Jane Austen. What would we say today?

Shall not you put them into our own room?
Mr Murray's letter is come.

I think we'd say 'Won't you put them in our room?' and 'Mr Murray's letter has come.'

It takes a while for a change in grammar to spread throughout society. To begin with, just a few people use the new form, then a few more, and slowly it becomes the new way of talking and writing.

But, as with any new development, not everyone likes it. People who are used to the old way of talking often dislike the new usage. Indeed, they can get very, very cross about it, and try to persuade everyone not to use it – usually by writing letters to the newspapers or complaining to a broadcasting company every time they hear the new usage on the radio or television.

They're wasting their time, of course. A new usage arrives when most people in a society decide to use it. In the case of English, that means millions and millions of people. Writing a letter of complaint to the BBC might make you feel better, but it won't stop the change taking place.

Changes in pronunciation also take a while to spread throughout society, though they don't take as long as changes in grammar. If we listen to radio programmes that were made 50 or 60 years ago, we hear accents that aren't used any longer. And we can usually hear these changes when we listen to people from different generations: our pronunciation of some words is going to be different from that of our parents, and their pronunciation will be different from that of our grandparents.

Here's an example. How do you say the word 'schedule'? There are two possibilities in British English. One sounds like 'sked-youll'; that's the way the word is said in the USA. The other sounds like 'shed-youll', that's the traditional way it's said in Britain. But young people in Britain usually say 'sked-youll', these days. Most older people say 'shed-youll'. It's a change that's been taking place in English over the past few decades. One day, everyone in Britain will be saying 'sked-youll', and the 'shed' pronunciation will be forgotten.

While a change is taking place, people notice it, and – as with grammar – they may say they don't like the new usage. But after a while everyone gets used to the new way of saying something. That's what happened to 'balcony'. A couple of hundred years ago, people pronounced this word as 'bal-<u>coh</u>-nee', with the stress on 'coh'. If we'd been alive in the mid-nineteenth century, we'd have heard people arguing about which was the right pronunciation – that one, or the new fashionable pronunciation of '<u>bal</u>-conee'. A few decades later, and everyone was saying it in the new way. The old pronunciation was history.

The area of language which changes most slowly is the writing system – the way we spell, punctuate, and capitalize words. If we look at a book that was printed a century ago, we won't see many differences in the way the writer spelled words or punctuated sentences. But go back two or three hundred years, and we'll immediately notice some changes. What's distinctive about this next piece of writing? It's from a guide about how to write, published in 1786.

Imitate the best Examples, and have a constant Eye at your Copy.

It was the fashion in English in those days to write a noun with a capital letter – just as German does today. Gradually, writers stopped doing this. Today, we use capital letters in only a few places – at the beginning of a sentence, for the word 'I', and for the names of people, places, and so on. And sometimes also as a sort of joke – as when we are making A Very Special Point.

Here's an example from punctuation. If I'd been alive in 1900, I'd have got a letter with an address laid out like this:

Mr. David Crystal,
   22, New St.,
      London, W.C.1.

I'd be very surprised if I got a letter with an address looking like that today. Much more likely it would be like this:

Mr David Crystal
22 New St
London
WC1 2GG

There are no punctuation marks, and the left-hand margin is

straight. It's a popular style these days. People find it makes the writing look clean and crisp. Keeping punctuation to a minimum is the modern way.

Finally, an example of how we change the way we talk to each other, as the years go by. How do we say 'hello' to each other these days? How do we say 'goodbye'? 'Hi' has come to replace 'hello' for many younger people – and increasingly for older people too. And goodbye is often replaced by expressions such as 'bye', 'see you later', and 'ciao'. If we go further back in time, we see even greater differences. In Shakespeare's day, people said such things as 'farewell', 'fare you well' and 'adieu' (from French, pronounced 'add-you'). Or, if you wanted to be really flowery, 'I do commend me to you'. They also said 'goodbye', except it was in a form which shows the origin of this word – 'God bye', short for 'God be with you'.

Which is a good way to end this chapter.

HELLO?

New technology always brings new usages, but we soon get used to them. When the telephone was invented, people had to work out what to say when it rang. Some people said their name very loudly. Some said 'Hello?' Some said 'Who's this?' Some said their telephone number.

Eventually one kind of response became routine. In Britain, it was to say our telephone number. But responses vary according to circumstances. These days, especially on mobile phones, people often say 'Hello?' or 'Hi', or give their name. In an office, where everyone knows everyone else, the response might be a simple 'Yeah'. A phone call to a service company might produce a formula reply such as: 'Hello, this is Jane. How can I help you?'

Answering machines of course have their own rules. Messages can be very formal and polite or totally insane. I recently left a message on a machine where I was greeted by: 'Hello, this is Bugs Bunny. I'm not in right now …'

Don't expect other countries to do the same. In German, when the phone rings, people respond with their surname. In French, they usually say 'Allo?' In Italian, they say 'Pronto', meaning 'Ready'. And in Japanese the equivalent of 'Hello' is 'Moshi moshi'.

Language variation

We saw in Chapter 12 that a language isn't the same wherever it's spoken. It appears as different accents and dialects, telling us which country, or which part of a country, the speakers come from. This is an important way in which language varies. But it's not the only way.

In the opening chapters of this book we saw another kind of language variation – in terms of age. If we listened to a recording of the voices of people aged from 1 to 100, it would be possible to guess roughly how old they were. We wouldn't get it exactly right, of course. But we'd be able to tell that Voice A was a little child, Voice B was a teenager, Voice C was middle-aged, Voice D was very old, and so on.

How can we tell? The main clue is the sound quality of the voice. Young people have high-pitched voices, as we saw in Chapter 4. Then, during their teens, the voice 'breaks', becoming deeper and more resonant. The voice matures further during our twenties and thirties. And in old age, it becomes weaker and huskier, because the muscles controlling the lungs and vocal folds don't work so efficiently.

There are other clues to how old we are. If, in one of our recordings, the speaker said 'That's wicked!' (meaning 'excellent'), how old would that person be? It's likely to be a young person, because 'wicked' has taken on this meaning among young people only in recent years. On the other hand, if we heard the speaker say 'That's nifty' (also meaning 'excellent'), it's likely to be an old person, as this was a really popular expression about 60 years ago. Our vocabulary, pronunciation, and grammar often give clues to how old we are. And conversational practices do too. Grandson might greet grandad with a 'Hi!' but he'll probably get a 'Hello' in return.

Probably the most obvious way in which language varies is to show the difference between the sexes. It's usually possible, from listening to a voice, to tell whether its owner is male or female. The pitch of the voice is a giveaway – high for women, low for men – though we occasionally get a surprise, because some men have high-pitched voices and some women have low-pitched voices.

In a few languages, also, the way men talk is different from the way women talk. In Japanese, for instance, there are certain words and sentences that only males use, and certain words and sentences that only females use. If you were in a school in Japan, and saw a message on a notice board which read 'boku ...', you'd know it would probably have been written by a boy, because that's the word boys use for 'I'. If a girl had written the message it would probably have been 'watashi'. I have to say 'probably', of course, because it's always possible for a girl who's a bit of a tomboy to say 'boku'. But normally, the two forms are used differently by the two sexes.

There's nothing like this in English. Boys and girls both use 'I'. There's no single bit of grammar or vocabulary which is *only* used by boys or *only* used by girls. A few words are more likely to be used by one sex or the other, of course. Girls are much more likely to use 'so', for example – in sentences like 'We were so busy'. They're more likely to use such words as 'lovely' and 'super', and such exclamations as 'Goodness me' or 'Oh dear'. But these are just trends. It's perfectly possible for boys to say 'Oh dear', and they often do.

The way we speak can also tell other people about the ethnic group we belong to – whether we're white or black or something else, or whether our family comes from South Asia or the Caribbean or Africa, or elsewhere. People are very proud of their roots, and they often develop ways of communicating which signal what those roots are.

The speech used by many black people in the USA and the Caribbean is a good example. We'll often hear such sentences as these, which show a different grammar from what is usual in standard English:

> She go by bus. (Standard English: She goes by bus.)
> They fine. (Standard English: They are fine.)
> We be done washed the car soon. (Standard English: We will have washed the car soon.)

Not all black people use these sentence patterns, and not all use them in exactly the same way. But it's unusual to find white people using them.

Notice that these aren't usages which signal regional dialects. Two people can have lived all their lives in the same city in Alabama in southern USA, but one says 'We be done washed' and the other says 'We will have washed'. They both speak American English from Alabama. But the kind of English they speak is different, because one is black and the other is white.

We met another kind of language variation in Chapters 10, 11, and 12, when we talked about the differences between upper-class and lower-class speech. All societies contain people who are 'high up' – the monarchs, presidents, and nobles, and those who have powerful jobs, such as in government and business. And all societies contain people who are 'low down' – with poor education, little money, and no power. In between, there may be other classes of people, in some countries recognized by the way they dress or behave, or by the jobs they do – or, of course, by the way they use language.

Language is a very powerful marker of the social class someone belongs to. If there are clear class divisions in a society, they will be reflected in the way people use language. For example, some will have a 'posh' accent. And those with a good education will speak and write the form of the language that is felt to be the 'best' – standard English, in the case of English-speaking countries.

In the days when the divisions in British society were very noticeable, it only took a single word to show which class you belonged to. If you were upper-class, you said 'lavatory paper'; if you weren't you said 'toilet paper'. Upper-class people had 'luncheon', looked at themselves in a 'looking glass', and ate their 'vegetables'. Everyone else had 'dinner', looked at themselves in a 'mirror', and ate their 'greens'. Distinctions of this kind still exist today, but they are much less noticeable because the divide between the upper and lower classes isn't as clear or as widespread as it used to be.

Another kind of language variation shows the relationships people have with each other.. How do we talk to people when we meet them? It all depends on how well we know them, and what our relationship is to them. If they're friends, we'll talk to them in a familiar way. If they're close friends, we'll be even more intimate. And if we don't know them at all, we'll be more distant and formal.

A good clue to the nature of a relationship is how we name each other. Imagine meeting someone called John Williams. We have the option of addressing him in several ways, and each way would say something about the links between us. Some are personal, some are professional.

Hello, Mr Williams
Hello, John
Hello, Johnnie
Hello, Williams
Hello, J W
Hello, Nobber

Presumably, in the last case, we are *very* old friends!

Several languages vary their 'you' words to show the nature of the relationship between people. In French, for example, we have the choice of saying 'tu' or 'vous', depending on how close we are to each other: 'vous' is the normal polite way of addressing someone;

'tu' is used when we know them well. It's always a special moment, in French, when two people feel they can say 'tu' to each other.

We make similar choices when we write to one another – such as when we decide how to begin and end a letter or an email. What would these beginnings to letters tell us about the relationship between the writer and reader?

Dear Jane
Dear Ms Smith
Dear Madam
Darling Jane
Yo, Janie baby

The first one is the ordinary polite way. The second is more formal. The third is very impersonal – probably a computer sent the letter! The fourth is intimate. And the last is 'good mates'.

Finally, the way we speak or write is also influenced by the actual situation in which we find ourselves. In a noisy place, we have to speak louder in order to be heard. In a church service, ministers adopt a special tone of voice. On the radio, announcers have to speak more slowly than they would in everyday conversation.

Sometimes the setting makes us use a special way of talking. In a law court, for instance, people have to address the judge in a certain way, saying 'm'lud' ('my lord') in Britain or 'your honor' in the USA. In the British Parliament, politicians traditionally refer to each other using special phrases. It wouldn't be correct to say 'As Michael White has just said …' It has to be 'As my Honourable Friend has just said …' (if they belong to the same political party) or 'As the Honourable Gentleman has just said …' (if they do not).

The written language is also very much affected by the setting, especially the way it is laid out on a page or screen. The headlines of a newspaper are set in very large type, so that people don't miss the stories. In the same way, if you're writing a poster to advertise an event in school, you need to make the letters large enough to be easily seen. And when people are advertising something, they make careful use of colours, spacing, and the size and shape of the letters and punctuation marks, to make the language suit the product. Which style best suits these two ads, for instance?

YE OLD TEA SHOPPE

YE OLD TEA SHOPPE

TAKE OFF WITH FASTAIR TODAY

TAKE OFF WITH FASTAIR TODAY

I don't think I'd like to travel with an airline which looked so ancient!

WHAT TIME IS IT?

It's Saturday evening at 10 o'clock, and you want to talk about what you did 12 hours before. You'll say something like this:

I went to the shops this morning.

But tune in to one of the international television channels, such as the BBC World Service or CNN, and you'll hear something different. It's still Saturday, but the newsreader will say:

President Obama was in New York Saturday morning.

You won't hear:

President Obama was in New York this morning.

This is because the programme is being broadcast in many parts of the world, where the time zones are different. In some places, it will already be Sunday morning, so to say 'this morning' could be ambiguous. It's another example of where the setting influences the nature of the language we use – though in this case the change is caused by our sense of time, not of place.

CHAPTER 23

Language at work

We see even more variation when we look at the way language is used in the workplace.

Next time you're in a school library, notice how the books are organized. There are sections such as BIOLOGY and HISTORY and GEOGRAPHY and RELIGION and LITERATURE and SCIENCE. It's the same in a public library – except that there are more headings there. You'll find LAW and MEDICINE, for instance, which aren't usually taught in school.

Pick a book from two of these sections – literature and science, for example – and open them somewhere in the middle. Choose a paragraph and read it. You don't have to understand *what* the writers are saying. Just notice *the way* they're saying it. You'll see differences like this:

Harry glanced into the cracked, dusty mirror and saw Ron and Hermione exchanging sceptical looks behind his back.

Cirrus clouds are found at high altitudes, at around 6,000 metres (20,000 feet), but can be at a much lower height in cold polar regions.

The style of the writing feels very different. Why?

It's because the writers are aiming to do different things. In the first example, we're being told an exciting story, so we see words which create a dramatic atmosphere, such as 'cracked' and 'dusty'. We see the names of the characters who are keeping the story moving along. And we see a new twist in the plot: *why* are Ron and Hermione looking at each other? It makes us want to read on.

In the second example, there are no names, no atmospheric words, no story twists. We're simply told some basic facts, briefly and accurately. In a word, it's scientific. We're given some knowledge, without any drama. We can read on if we like, but we don't feel we have to.

We can feel the difference between the two styles if we mix them up. What would you make of this?

Harry finished his cornflakes and found cirrus clouds at high altitudes, at around 6,000 metres (20,000 feet), but Hermione, who was wearing a red dress, thought they could be at a much lower height in cold polar regions.

This sounds very strange. It doesn't sound scientific any more. Why not?

It's because, when we write about science, it doesn't matter who people are, or what they're wearing, or what they had for breakfast. It's a fact that cirrus clouds exist at 6,000 metres, regardless of whether Harry found them there or not. It's a fact that they are lower in polar regions, whatever Hermione thinks. Their personal opinion is beside the point. And cirrus clouds would still exist at 6,000 metres even if she was wearing a blue dress or if Harry had eaten toast for breakfast.

In scientific language, sentences say that an activity is taking place without telling us anything about the people who are performing the activity. Scientists write like the second sentence below, not the first:

Harry found cirrus clouds at high altitudes. (We know who found them.)

Cirrus clouds are found at high altitudes. (We don't know who found them.)

This is a kind of language we call 'impersonal'.

Nor do we let our imagination take over, when we try to write scientifically. We won't read this sort of thing in a science book:

Cirrus clouds are really beautiful and they make me tingle all over whenever I see them, and they are found at high altitudes.

Science doesn't care about our feelings. One person might find clouds beautiful and tingly. Another person might not. But it's a fact that they are found at high altitudes, and science aims to state the facts. If you want to find out about how people feel, you're better off reading a poem or a novel.

We can sum all these examples up by saying that scientific language is not like other kinds of language. It uses special words and grammar to describe and explain the nature of the universe, often with lots of technical symbols and diagrams. If you train to be a scientist, one of the first things you have to do is learn to speak and write in a scientific way. It's a bit like learning a new language.

The same point applies to all the other jobs in life. If you want to be a lawyer, or a doctor, or a religious minister, or a radio presenter, or a sports commentator, you have to learn a new kind of language. Every job has its special words (or 'jargon') and grammar, and its own way of talking or writing. Think about all the sports commentators on radio or television, and how their style alters depending on the sport they're describing. A football game sounds very different from a horse race or a tennis match. The speed and loudness of the commentator's voice are very different, for a start. Even if you're a long way from the television, you can often tell what kind of sport is on just from listening to the tone of voice.

The jobs people have bring us into contact with a new kind of language variation. We can talk about 'scientific English', 'religious

English', 'medical English', and so on. These varieties are like the dialects and accents we talked about in Chapter 12, except that the language doesn't tell us where people are from, but what job they do. They're often called *occupational dialects*, for that reason.

As we grow up, we learn more and more about occupational dialects. Just by watching television, we learn about the way policemen, lawyers, doctors, and all sorts of other people speak. If we go to a church, or a mosque, or some other religious setting, we experience the very distinctive kinds of language used there. Out and about, we hear people in shops, markets, and fairgrounds using their own kind of language to sell us things. We hear announcers on trains, boats, and planes using their own kind of language to tell us things. Even by the age of 10, we've picked up an awful lot about the way a job can make us change the way we speak or write.

You can test your knowledge of occupational dialects. Here's a selection of sentences from people in different jobs. See if you can match the sentences with the job-names. (I'll give you the answers at the end of the chapter.)

Test 1

1 Thou knowest how much we love Thee.   **A** football commentator

2 I put it to you that you are lying.   **B** army sergeant

3 They thought it was all over
   – but it isn't!   **C** advertiser

4 Stand up straight, you horrible
   little man!   **D** scientist

5 Atoms combine to form units called
   molecules.   **E** lawyer

6 You are not obliged to say anything.   **F** priest

7 These are yummy delicious!   **G** police officer

We can do a test like this with sets of single words, too. Which jobs do you think these words belong to? Again, match the sets with the job-names.

Test 2

1 depression, cold front, precipitation, force 5	A hairdresser
2 holiday, destination, check-in, ticketing	B dentist
3 cavity, occlusion, decay, incisor	C estate agent
4 symptoms, diagnosis, pulse, medication	D weather-forecaster
5 amps, speakers, kit, deck, cans	E travel agent
6 salon, blow dry, shampoo, set, trim	F doctor
7 offer, sale, detached, buyer, attractive	G disc jockey

There's something interesting about one of the words in line 5 of Test 2. 'Cans'. I could have used the word 'headphones' instead. But people who have jobs in broadcasting usually talk about 'cans' rather than 'headphones' when they're talking to each other. It's part of broadcasting slang. And slang, as we'll see, turns out to be one of the most important ways in which we can vary our speech.

ANSWERS
Test 1: 1F; 2E; 3A; 4B; 5D; 6G; 7C
Test 2: 1D; 2E; 3B; 4F; 5G; 6A; 7C

LANGUAGE IN CODE

Sometimes a task produces a very abbreviated form of language. It becomes a kind of code, and only those who take the trouble to learn the code can understand what is going on. Do you recognize any of these?

1 P-Q4, N-KB3, NxP

2 K1, K2tog, K5, Cr2R

3 H_2SO_4, CH_3, H_2O

4 ax2 + bx + c = 0

5 <i>, </i>, ,

Here we have examples from (1) chess, (2) knitting, (3) chemistry, (4) mathematics, and (5) computing. If you've learned these subjects, you'll be able to interpret the symbols. If you haven't, the examples will look like foreign languages.

Here are some translations. 'P-Q4' means 'move Pawn to the fourth square on the Queen's row'. 'K5' means 'knit five stitches'. 'H_2O' is the chemical formula for water. The letters in a mathematical formula stand for unknown numbers. <i> and </i> are used in a type of computer programming known as HTML, when you want to have a word print out in italics. The <i> tells the computer that it should start using italics, and the same letter with a </> before it tells the computer to stop. If you typed '<i>hello</i> there', the words would appear on a page as '*hello* there'.

CHAPTER 24

Slang

What do you make of this conversation?

> Bill: I'm gonna take the Porker down to the bakery for some
> rolls.
> Ben: I'll come with you, man. I need some juice for my Pug
> too.

It sounds very odd. Somebody taking a pig to a shop to get it some
bread? And buying fruit juice for a dog?

But it's only odd if we don't realize that this is a special kind of
'cool' language used by some people who are mad keen on cars. To
understand it, we need to translate the words like this:

Porker	Porsche
bakery	petrol/gas station
rolls	petrol/gas
juice	petrol/gas
Pug	Peugeot

The world of cars is full of words like this. Here are some more:

shoes	wheels

windair	conditioning
boots	tyres
Roller	Rolls Royce
Landy	Land Rover

So now you should be able to understand this next sentence:

I need new boots for the shoes on my Landy.

Words like 'shoes' and 'bakery' are part of automobile slang.
What is slang? There's an old rhyme which goes like this:

The chief use of slang
Is to show you're one of the gang.

This doesn't mean 'gang' in the sense of a band of youths or criminals who fight in the streets. It means a group of people who have the same kind of interests and background. There are hundreds of different kinds of slang in a language. When a group of doctors get together to talk shop, we could say they form a sort of gang. So do a group of lawyers or footballers or teachers. And if we listened to the members of one of these gangs talking to each other, we'd hear them use lots of words that belong only in their world.

How do I know about these words? Do I belong to the world of cool racers and hot rods? Well, actually, no. So when I talk about cars, I don't myself use such words as 'bakery' and 'shoes'. But as a linguist I keep my ears open, and hear these words in the cinema and on television. And I keep my eyes open too. There are several internet sites which provide lists of auto slang, compiled by the people who do use these words every day.

Linguists love collecting slang. It's a bit like collecting stamps – or maybe birdwatching would be a better comparison. Listen! There's a new word I haven't heard before! What does it mean? Who uses it? I'll write it down in my notebook. I remember going to the doctor's a few years ago, and as he wrote out a prescription for some medicine he muttered: 'I think you'd better have some bug-juice'. I wrote that down as soon as I left the surgery. He meant 'antibiotics'.

'Bug-juice' is a piece of medical slang. Normally, doctors would use it only when talking to other medical people. So why did he use it to me? I'm not a doctor. Probably it was because we were friends and had a similar background. When people have a lot in common, they share their slang with each other.

Slang is actually quite difficult for linguists to find out about. You will have your local slang that you use in your school or in your town, and there's no way I would ever know about it unless you told me what it was. Indeed, in your area you'll probably have several different kinds of slang. The slang that kids use in primary school is likely to be different from what is used in secondary school. If your town has several schools, there are often differences in the kind of slang heard in each school. And there may even be words that are used differently within a single school. I once worked with a group of students in the final year of senior school, who listened out for the slang used in their school. They found that the slang used by first-year students was very different from their own.

That's one of the things about slang. It changes so quickly. Words that are 'in' this year might be 'out' next year. Here are some of the slang words that were in fashion a few years ago. Do you still use them now?

bling	fancy jewellery
bones	money
phat	cool, great
sup, wassup	what's up?
wicked	cool, great
yo	hello

And here are some of the slang words that were used back in the 1960s and 1970s:

| blast | great time |
| bread | money |

bug	irritate
dig?	understand?
fab	fabulous, fantastic
far out	excellent
funky	neat, cool
groovy	great, cool
pad	house, home

You may know some of these words because you've heard older people use them, or perhaps you've seen a movie (such as *Grease*) where some of them turn up. And maybe you use one or two yourselves. But most of them belong to 40 years ago.

The further back in time we go, the more difficult it is to understand the slang people use. In Victorian England, people on the street would talk about a 'billy' (a handkerchief), a 'dipper' (a pickpocket), and 'luggers' (earrings). And what do you think the innkeeper means when he calls his friend a 'bully rook' in Shakespeare's play *The Merry Wives of Windsor*? That was slang in the sixteenth century for a 'fine fellow'.

Some linguists have been very daring, in tracking down slang. One scholar, Eric Partridge, used to go into the back streets of London and ask shady characters about the kind of slang they used. A gun, for instance, might be called a 'cannon', a 'rod', a 'heater', or other less obvious names, such as a 'biscuit'. I'm glad he lived to tell the tale!

It's less dangerous to explore home-grown slang. Most households have made-up words that are known only by the members of the family, or their close friends and relatives. For instance, do you have a special name in your house for the remote control that changes the channels on your TV? Here are just a few of the pet names that people have used for this device:

bimmer	pinger
blapper	plinky
dibber	podger
donker	pringer

dooberry	splonker
flicker	woojit

A collection of these family words was published in 2008. The editors called their book *Kitchen Table Lingo*.

Slang is used by people who want to show, by the way they talk, that they belong together. It's very informal, casual, colloquial. It's like a secret language, known only to the people who are members of the group. It's therefore very different from the standard use of a language, as I described it in Chapter 10. A standard language, like Standard English, uses words that are there for everyone to use. If we want our speech and writing to be understood by as many people as possible, we have to avoid slang.

When we learn a language, then, one of the things we need to do is learn which words are standard and which are slang. And we need to remember not to mix them up. It's natural and normal to use slang when talking with our friends. If we didn't, and used only standard English, they'd think us a bit weird. But equally, we should avoid slang when we're talking to a general audience. We won't hear BBC or CNN announcers using slang, for instance, because they need to have their language understood by all their listeners.

And it's especially important not to use slang when writing something that's going to be read by people who don't belong to your own little group. If you forget this, you can get into trouble. If you put slang words into a school essay, for instance, don't be surprised to get it back with the words corrected. This will be another reason (along with the one I mentioned on p.68) why you'll get low marks.

We won't find slang words in print – unless, of course, the writer is deliberately trying to show how people talk, as in a crime novel. Just occasionally, in this book, you'll see me use a slang expression – and when I do, I put it in inverted commas, to show that it's a special usage. You'll see an example if you look back at the second paragraph of this chapter. And there's another one coming up in the middle of Chapter 25.

WOULD YOU ADAM AND EVE IT?

About 200 years ago, people living in the East End of London (Cockneys) began to use rhyming phrases to replace certain words. Instead of saying 'feet', they said 'plates of meat'. Instead of saying 'stairs', they said 'apples and pears'. So you might hear sentences like this:

I hurt my plates of meat coming down the apples and pears.

Why did they do it? Probably just for fun. But criminals also used such phrases to make it difficult for the police to understand what they were saying.

Here are some other examples of what is called 'rhyming slang'.

Hampstead Heath	teeth
lump of lead	head
artful dodger	lodger
lean and lurch	church
Adam and Eve	believe

The process of making up new rhymes still goes on today. What do you think these mean?

He's on the Adrian Mole.
I want an Ali G.
She was wearing her Barack Obamas.

I don't know whether these are used very often, but they've all been invented just in the last few years.

Answers: He's on the dole.
          I want a pee.
          She was wearing her pyjamas.

CHAPTER 25

Dictionaries

Here's a challenge. Answer these questions.

1. When you're at home, where do you keep your mobile phone?
2. Do you understand how your mobile phone works?
3. How often do you use your mobile phone?
4. When did you last upgrade your mobile phone?

I suspect you're thinking: 'Not much of a challenge'. So here's another one.

1. When you're at home, where do you keep your dictionary?
2. Do you understand how your dictionary works?
3. How often do you use your dictionary?
4. When did you last upgrade your dictionary?

Most people find those questions much harder to answer. Here's one set of responses:

1. I'm not sure. It's on a shelf in the sitting room – I think!
2. Not really.
3. Only when I'm doing crossword puzzles or playing Scrabble.
4. I can't remember.

What would your answers be? Here are mine.

1. One is on my desk right next to my computer. Another is in my Online Favourites.
2. Yes, I've read the introduction at the front of the dictionary, which tells me all about how it was written.
3. Almost every day.
4. This year.

You might be surprised by my answer to Question 3. You might think: David Crystal has been studying the English language for years and years. Why should he ever need to look anything up in a dictionary? Surely he knows all there is to know about words?

I wish I did! But check back to the end of Chapter 3, when I asked 'How many words do we know?' For me, the answer is around 100,000. That's quite a lot, but it's only a tenth of the words in the English language. English has over a million words. Most of them are words to do with science and technology, which I don't know and probably will never need to know. But every now and then I come across one of these words, and need to look up what it means. That's when I need my dictionary.

The other day, for instance, I was reading a story where the writer was doing some rock climbing and said he had put his foot in a 'grike' to help him up a slope. I had no idea what it meant. Was it some sort of footwear? Or a climbing tool of some kind? The temptation is to think 'It doesn't matter – I've got a rough idea', and to carry on reading. Fight against that temptation! Always look the word up. I did, and found it was nothing to do with shoes or tools. A grike is a crack in a rock which has been made larger by the rain.

That's one more word added to my vocabulary. If I knew 100,000 words before, now I know 100,001. That's a good feeling. To use a bit of slang I learned when I lived in Liverpool: I felt 'dead chuffed' – really pleased with myself. If you're interested in language – and if you've read this far in the book, you must be – whenever you learn a new word you should feel dead chuffed too.

Another time I use my dictionary is when I *think* I know what a word means, but am not exactly sure. In another piece of recent reading, I came across the phrase 'flexor muscle'. What sort of muscle was that? I knew the word 'flex', which means 'bend', so I assumed this was a muscle which made some part of the body bend. But which part? I wasn't sure. So I checked, and the answer was – any part. A flexor muscle is one which moves *any* joint or limb.

It's very important to pay attention to every part of a dictionary definition, if we want to use a word correctly. If we don't, it's easy to confuse people by saying something we don't mean. Take the word 'aftermath'. Here's one dictionary definition:

The effects arising from an (especially unpleasant) event.

So people say such things as this:

The film was about the aftermath of the war in the Middle East.
Traffic was held up for several hours in the aftermath of the accident.

Now here's an example of what someone once wrote in a school essay.

The church fete was great fun and very successful, and in the aftermath a thousand pounds was given to charity.

There's something wrong with this. The definition says that the event is usually an 'unpleasant' one. So if we write 'In the aftermath of the church fete', it suggests that the event was a disaster – maybe because a tornado had blown all the tents down! But here there was no disaster; the fete was a very enjoyable and successful event. So the writer was wrong to use the word 'aftermath'. He should have written something like this:

The church fete was great fun and very successful, and as a result a thousand pounds was given to charity.

If he'd bothered to look the word up in a dictionary, he might have avoided the problem.

What other uses does a dictionary have? Many people use it to check their spellings, especially when they're in the early stages of learning a language. That's one of the chief reasons students in school use a dictionary. Another use is to check how a word is pronounced. The other day I came across the word 'telemeter' in a book, and I realized that I had no idea how to say it aloud. A telemeter is a device for recording data that are some distance away. But how do people say it?

Is it 'tell-y – meet – er', with the stress on the first syllable?
Or 'te – lem – iter', with the stress on the second syllable?

My dictionary told me that both pronunciations are heard, but the first one is used more often.

The dictionary gives us other kinds of information too. It will tell us something about the grammar of a word – whether it is a noun, or a verb, or some other part of speech. It will tell us whether a word is used in a special way – whether it's found in medicine or law, for instance, or whether it's an old-fashioned word or a rude word. It will also give us examples of the way the word is used in sentences: in the best dictionaries, we'll see several examples like the ones I used above for 'aftermath'. And it will give us information about the history and origin of words – how they came into the language and how they've changed over the centuries. This is the subject of *etymology*, and it's so fascinating that I'm going to spend the whole of the next chapter on it.

So that's it, then? We've found our dictionary, discovered the kind of information it contains, and started to use it regularly. Anything else? Don't forget question 4. Is it up-to-date?

New editions of a dictionary come out every few years, and to have only an old one in the house is a bit like having an ancient mobile phone. We're missing out on all the latest features and applications. If the dictionary is 10 years old, for instance, just think of the thousands of words and senses it won't contain – such as all the words to do with the internet. Also, dictionary-writers are always thinking of new ways of presenting the information, to make the books easier to use. Some dictionaries now have CDs at the back, containing lots of extra material. And many dictionaries can also be accessed online. Whatever dictionary we buy, we need to trade it in for a new one every five years or so.

There are two other things you need to know about dictionary-writing. It's called *lexicography*. And the people who write dictionaries are called *lexicographers*, like Noah Webster and Samuel Johnson, whom we met when we were talking about spelling in Chapter 10. If you want to find out more information about those words, you know what you can do: look them up in a dictionary.

WORD DISPLAYS

A dictionary is the main kind of book that tells us about the vocabulary of a language, but it's not the only one. A *thesaurus* is another kind of word book, but it does a different job. A thesaurus brings words together which have a similar meaning.

Imagine you're writing a story about someone who walked through a field and got very dirty. You could say they were 'dirty', but you want to make your story more interesting, so you rack your brains trying to think of other words with a similar meaning. You might come up with some by yourself – but if you don't, you can get some ideas from looking 'dirty' up in a thesaurus. There you would find an entry like this:

dirty filthy, foul, muddy, mucky, soiled, grimy, messy, swampy, sodden

Now you can choose which word best suits what you want to say.

A thesaurus is the opposite of a dictionary. When we use a dictionary, we have a word in our head and we want to look up its meaning. When we use a thesaurus, we have a meaning in our head, and we want to look up which word best expresses it.

Computers now allow us to display words in all kinds of interesting ways. When we use a piece of software such as Wordle (www.wordle.net), we can see all the words in a piece of work displayed as a 'cloud'. The size of a word reflects how often it's used. I put the entire text of this book into Wordle, and this is what came out. The word-cloud gives a good impression of the content of this book. You'd expect 'language' to be largest. But did you expect 'people'? I wasn't surprised. There can be no language without people, and no people without language.

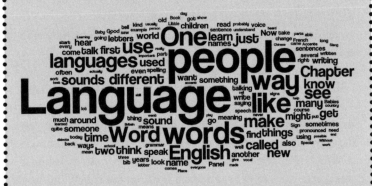

CHAPTER 26

Etymology

Etymology is the study of the history and origins of words, and it's a subject that is full of surprises. Take the words 'salary' and 'sausage'. These days they have completely different meanings.

A salary is the amount of money someone is paid in a year for doing a job.
A sausage is a type of food made of meat shaped into a thin roll.

But once upon a time they were the same word. How can that be?

'Salary' came into English in the fourteenth century. It comes from the Latin word 'salarium', which meant 'salt-money'. Roman soldiers were given money especially to buy salt, which was a very important substance, as it helped to preserve food. 'Sausage' also arrived in English in the fourteenth century, coming from another Latin word 'salsicium', which meant something made from 'salted meat'. The common element in the two words is 'sal', which is the Latin word for 'salt'.

Several other English words have their origins in salt. 'Sauce' is one. This was 'salsa' in Latin, meaning that something was 'salted'. 'Salad' is another, coming from 'salata' in Latin, also meaning 'salted'. Over the centuries, these words have changed their meaning so that they now refer to very different things. People have sauce on their salad and their sausages, and pay for it with their salary.

Every word in a language has a history, and dictionaries tell us what that is. Let's stay with food. They will tell us, for example, that:

'melon' comes from French; it arrived in English in the late 1300s

'potato' comes from Spanish; it arrived in English in the mid-1500s

'yoghurt' comes from Turkish; it arrived in English in the early 1600s

'spaghetti' comes from Italian; it arrived in English in the mid-1800s

'sushi' comes from Japanese; it arrived in English in the late 1800s

These are all words which have kept the same meaning since they arrived in the language. The potatoes that were first eaten when Shakespeare was alive are the same sort of vegetable as the potatoes we eat today.

Many other words have changed their meaning since arriving in English. Today, if we say that someone is 'silly', we mean that they are foolish or stupid, often in a funny sort of way. But 1,000 years ago it didn't mean this at all. When the word was first used in English it meant 'happy' or 'blessed'. Then it developed the meaning of 'innocent'. Later still it meant someone who deserves our pity because there's something wrong with them. To say that someone was 'silly' meant that they were feeble-minded. These days, of course, we can be silly even though we're intelligent.

Words continue to change their meaning today. Here are some examples from the world of the internet:

- A 'mouse' has been a kind of small animal for over 1,000 years, but since the 1960s it has also come to mean a hand-held device to control a pointer on a computer screen.

- 'Spam' was originally a kind of tinned meat, but since the early 1990s it has come to mean unwanted email messages.
- To 'surf' originally meant to ride on a surfboard, but since the early 1990s it has also come to mean moving from site to site on the internet.

And of course many of the slang words discussed in Chapter 24 have come into existence through a change of meaning, such as 'wicked' and 'cool'.

Sometimes words change their meaning in ways which make us think about them very differently. When I was a boy, the only sense of 'cowboy' that I knew was the one in films, where there were 'cowboys and indians'. The cowboys were always the good guys. But since the 1970s, another meaning has come along. If we hear someone talk about 'cowboy builders', that's not nice. They're people who don't have the right skills and who do inferior work. Today, cowboys are the bad guys.

That's an example of a word taking on a bad meaning. We find the opposite type of change taking place too: words taking on a good meaning. 'Nice' is an example. This word came into the language in the 1300s meaning 'foolish' or 'ignorant'. It later developed other negative meanings, such as 'showy', 'fussy', or 'lazy'. But gradually other senses developed. To be 'nice' could mean that you were 'well-dressed' or you were 'particular' or 'careful' about things. In the 1700s it developed a wide range of positive meanings, such as 'agreeable', 'pleasant', 'kind', and attractive', and these are the ones we have today.

Words also change by becoming more general in meaning. When 'office' first came into English, in the late 1200s, it meant a particular kind of religious service. Only people such as priests and nuns had an office, which they followed every day. Today, the word has a much more general range of meaning. It can mean any kind of official position or duty, or a room where people carry out administrative tasks. We say things like:

Mary's office is in the City.

John works in the Foreign Office.

She holds a high office in the government.

The word still has its religious meaning, but that is only one small part of its use today.

The opposite type of change is when words become less general in meaning. Their sense narrows. In Old English, the word 'mete' (spelled 'meat' today) meant any kind of solid food. Today, 'meat' is restricted to the flesh of certain kinds of animals. Only occasionally do we find a word which keeps the older meaning. When people talk about 'sweetmeats', for instance, they're referring to such things as candied sweets and sugared nuts. That's nothing to do with animal flesh. Nor is 'mincemeat' (as used in mince pies) anything to do with animals. But these are exceptions. Only a small part of the original meaning of 'meat' is used today.

As we saw in Chapter 21, we have to keep a wary eye open for these changes of sense when we read books written many years ago. We must be careful not to read in the modern meaning. For example, when we read in a Shakespeare play that someone was 'naughty', we might think that this word had the same meaning as it has today. In fact, it's very different. To say that a little boy is being naughty today means that he's being badly behaved – a bit of a mischief. But if characters in Shakespeare are called 'naughty', it means much more than that. They are being truly wicked or evil.

The scholars who study etymologies are called *etymologists*. And there's plenty of research for them to do, because many words are mysteries. We have no idea where they came from. Take 'jam', for instance – the stuff we put on bread. Why do we call it 'jam'? Jam is made from fruit which has been boiled along with sugar until it is a nice messy spread. Did people originally call it 'jam' because they thought of the fruit being crushed or 'jammed' down into a pulp? I think so, but we don't know for sure.

There are hundreds of words like this. Nobody knows where the word 'bap' (meaning a bread roll) came from. Nobody knows why scientists are called 'boffins'. Nobody knows why people who do crazy things are said to be 'bonkers'. Is it because they're acting as if they've had a 'bonk' on the head? Etymologists try to find the answers to these questions.

All words have a history – and that includes the names of people and places. We won't find these in a dictionary because they exist outside of a language. We might know such names as 'Paris', 'Bordeaux', and 'François', but that doesn't mean we can speak French! And similarly, people who speak other languages can talk happily about such names as 'David', 'Elizabeth', 'Manchester', and 'Kentucky' without knowing a word of English. Nonetheless, we can still study the history of these names. And when we do, we find that every name has a story to tell.

BEING A GROOM

The study of a word's history can also help explain why some words appear to be strange. Take the word 'groom', as in 'bridegroom'. Why is it 'groom'? A groom is someone who is an employee, especially one who looks after horses. What's it got to do with getting married? A bridegroom isn't the bride's servant. Nor is he someone who is going to clean his wife's skin and hair to make her look smart! So why is he called a groom? Etymology can give us the answer.

When the word was first used in English, it was actually different in form. It was 'bridgome', pronounced 'breed-go-muh'. The first part, 'brid', meant 'bride'. And the second part, 'gome', meant 'man'. 'Gome' was a word which was used a lot in Old English, but people stopped using it during the Middle Ages. By the 1500s, nobody knew what a 'gome' was. So they replaced it with a more familiar word which had the same sort of sound, 'groom'. 'Bridgome' became 'bridegroom'.

People do this quite a lot. If they don't understand a word, they simply change it to make it sound more intelligible. When the word 'cucaracha' came into English from Spanish in the early 1600s, people must have found it very strange, because they soon altered it to the more friendly-sounding 'cockroach', even though a cockroach has nothing at all to do with cockerels. Nor does 'sparrow-grass' (a colloquial name for 'asparagus') have anything to do with sparrows.

CHAPTER 27

Place names

We need to give names to places so that we can tell people where we live and find our way around. Imagine what it would be like without any place names. We'd have to say something like this:

> Come and see me tomorrow. I live in a small town five miles from where you live. You get to it by travelling north along the main road, passing three settlements, until you get to a hill, then at the top of a hill you'll see another settlement by some trees. Take the first turning on the left, and you'll see a street with lots of houses. Our is the second house on the right.

It's much easier to say:

> Come and see me tomorrow. I live in Leethorpe. You get to it by travelling north from Redcliff. As you enter Leethorpe, the first on the left is Bridge Road. I live at number 4.

Or simply:

> Come and see me tomorrow. I live at 4 Bridge Road, Leethorpe, Bedfordshire.

We can then use a map or type the name into a sat nav, and find the place ourselves.

Where do places get their names from? Why is the county called Bedfordshire? Why is the town called Leethorpe? Why is the road called Bridge? People are always asking 'why' about place names, especially if the name is strange or funny. In the USA, for instance, there's a place called Hot Coffee. Why?

With many place names, the reason is obvious. They're named after people. Washington is named after the first president of the United States. Places like Georgetown, Williamsburg, Victoria, and Maryland are named after British kings and queens. St Albans is named after a saint. The city of Columbus in Ohio is named after the famous explorer.

Many places are named after obvious features of the landscape. It's no surprise to learn that Twin Peaks in the USA is located at a place where you can see two mountains. And it's easy to work out why these places have their names:

Salt Lake City, Table Mountain, Swan River, Westport, Newtown, Great North Road

So presumably Bridge Road crosses a bridge, or leads to a bridge.

But this is where things get interesting, because often we find a place like Bridge Road, and there's no sign of a bridge! Now we have to do some detective work. When was there a bridge? We can start asking people who have lived in the area for years, to see if they know. Or we can look on old maps, and see if they mention one.

We have to do some historical detective work with most place names, actually. Where did the name Hot Coffee come from? It turns out that in the late 1800s a man opened an inn along a highway in Mississippi and sold hot coffee to travellers. The sign outside said 'Hot Coffee'. Everyone remembered the place because of the drink, and started saying things like 'Let's stop at Hot Coffee'. Eventually the name came to be used, not just for the inn, but for all the farms and houses in the neighbourhood.

Sometimes the meaning of a place name is clear, but the event which caused the name is long forgotten. As we travel around the world we'll find such names as Cape Catastrophe, Fort Defiance, Skeleton Bay, and Foggy Island. There must have been skeletons around when explorers first arrived at Skeleton Bay in Africa, but nobody now knows who they belonged to.

Many names consist of two or more parts. Sometimes the meaning of each part is easy to work out:

Southport, Horsepath, Blackheath, Newcastle

But a name like Leethorpe isn't so obvious, because the two parts of the word don't have meanings we recognize in modern English. What is a 'lee'? What is a 'thorpe'? Once we know what these words meant in Old English, 1,000 years ago, the name starts to make sense. 'Lee' comes from an Old English word which meant a wood, or a clearing in a wood. 'Thorpe' comes from an Old English word which meant a village or farm. So if you lived in Leethorpe, in Anglo-Saxon times, you lived in a village built in a cleared area of woodland.

Here are three more elements we often see in town names:

- If a town ends in '-by', it was originally a farmstead or small village where some of the Viking invaders settled. The first part of the name sometimes referred to the person who owned the farm – Grimsby was 'Grim's village'. Derby was 'a village where deer were found'. The word 'by' still means 'town' in Danish.

- If a town ends in '-ing', it tells us about the people who lived there. Reading means 'the people of Reada', in other words 'Reada's family or tribe'. We don't know who Reada was, but his name means 'red one', so he probably had red hair.

- If a town ends in '-caster' or '-chester', it was originally a Roman fort or town. The word comes from a Latin word 'castra', meaning a camp or fortification. The first part of the name is usually the name of the locality where the fort was built. So Lancaster, for example, is 'the Roman fort on the River Lune'.

These names started out in Britain, but today they can be found anywhere in the English-speaking world. There are Lancasters in Australia and Canada, and several in the USA.

All kinds of places have names, from the largest location to the smallest. Here are some examples:

- planets – Venus was named after the Roman goddess of beauty and love.
- continents – America is named after an explorer, Amerigo Vespucci.
- countries – Wales comes from an Anglo-Saxon word meaning 'foreigners' or 'barbarians'.
- states – Kentucky comes from an American Indian language, Iroquois, meaning 'meadow land'.
- counties – Bedford is the river-crossing ('ford') where Beda lived.
- mountains – Everest was named after Sir George Everest, who first recorded its height and location.
- districts – Tottenham (in London) is 'Totta's homestead'.
- cities – Birmingham is 'the village of the family of Beorma'.
- towns – Ormskirk in Lancashire is 'Orm's church'.
- streets – Oxford Street in London is named after the second Earl of Oxford, who owned the land in the early 1700s.

This isn't a complete list. We give names to fields, rivers, valleys, hills, woods, and all sorts of other geographical features. We name shops, pubs, restaurants, theme parks, schools, colleges, farms, and all sorts of other buildings. Human beings love to name things.

And especially, people love to name the house they live in. This is a really interesting topic to research, because it's the one time that people have the chance to name a place for themselves. In all the other examples in this chapter, somebody else has thought up the name. But when people buy a house, they can give it a name themselves – or change the name if they don't like the one that's there already.

Many house names simply describe how they look or where they are, or what used to happen there. In a survey a few years ago, the top 20 most widely used house names in the UK were these:

1.	The Cottage	11.	The Barn
2.	Rose Cottage	12.	The Old Rectory
3.	The Bungalow	13.	Hillside
4.	The Coach House	14.	Hillcrest
5.	Orchard House	15.	The Croft
6.	The Lodge	16.	The Old Vicarage
7.	Woodlands	17.	Sunnyside
8.	The Old School House	18.	Orchard Cottage
9.	Ivy Cottage	19.	Yew Tree Cottage
10.	The Willows	20.	The Laurels

It sounds as if most of them are in country towns and villages. Trees and plants are very common in this list, as are names describing what the building used to be.

Other popular house names are based on animals:

Badger Cottage, Magpies, Robin's Nest

And quite a few names use favourite holiday destinations:

Windermere, Costa Brava, Naples

or names from favourite books:

Manderley, Rivendell, Bleak House

In Stratford-upon-Avon, several guest houses are named after

Shakespeare's plays. There's one called Twelfth Night.

Another popular strategy is to play with the language in some way. People often change the spelling of a word:

Faerie Glen, Kosy Korner, Dunroamin ('done roaming')

or make you read the name backwards:

Tivuli, Deroda, Tiedam

The names sometimes tell you who lives there:

Mikelynn, Billion (Bill + Marion), The Eddies (the family is called Edwards)

They may even use a foreign language:

Casa Nostra (Spanish for 'Our House'), Mon Repos (French for 'My Rest')

But the best names, I think, are those where we have no idea why the house has its name – until we ask. I know a house called The Chimes. Why? Because it belongs to a family called Bell. I know another house called Spooks. Why? It's next door to a cemetery. I know another one called Offbeat. Why? It's the home of a retired policeman.

Do ask. People love to tell the story behind their house name.

DISCWORLD ON EARTH

In 2009, two roads in a new housing development at Wincanton, Somerset, were given names from Terry Pratchett's *Discworld* stories. People were asked to vote from a shortlist of 14 names suggested by the author. Which ones would you have voted for?

Mollymog Street	**Lobbin Clout**
Moon Pond Lane	**Scoone Avenue**
Cable Street	**Tenth Egg Street**
Shamlegger Street	**Kicklebury Street**
Peach Pie Street	**Morpork Street**
Treacle Mine Road	**Ankh Street**
Hen and Chickens Field	**The Ridings**

The two winners were Peach Pie Street and Treacle Mine Road.

This isn't the first time a fantasy series has led to street names. In the small town of Grabowiecz in Poland you'll find Obi-Wan-Kenobi Street (it's Obi-Wana-Kenobiego in Polish). And in the town of Upper Marlboro, in Maryland, USA, several streets have been named after the characters in *Star Trek*. There's a Picard Lane, a Reiker Drive, a Laforge Lane, and a Crusher Court.

CHAPTER 28

Personal names

If there's one thing guaranteed to upset people, it's to spell their name wrong. And they go out of their way to make sure we don't. They say such things as:

> It's Anne with an 'e'.
> That's Taylor with a 'y' not an 'i'.
> It's Katherine with a 'k' and an 'e'.
> Hilary has one 'l' (not two, as in Hillary Clinton).

Our names are very special. Parents often spend a lot of time thinking what name to give their baby. And, once we've got our name, it takes a very important event indeed to make us change it.

We need some terminology in order to talk about names. There are three possibilities today.

- We have a *first name*, such as (English) Michael or Mary, or (French) Antoine or Amélie. This is sometimes called a *given name* or – for people with a Christian background – a *Christian name*.
- We have a *surname* or *family name*, such as (English) Smith, (German) Klein, or (Chinese) Wang. The surname that a woman is born with is called her *maiden name*.

- Many people have one or more *middle names*, such as Michael James Smith or Mary Catherine Jane Williams. In English, they often shorten the middle name to a single letter, such as Michael J. Smith – something which happens a lot in the USA.

Different languages have different naming habits. In the UK, if we met someone called Michael James Smith, he would usually be called Michael. But in Germany, if we met someone called Johann Wolfgang Schmidt, he would usually be called Wolfgang. Germans use a middle name as their 'call name' ('Rufname' in German – pronounced 'roof – nah – muh').

It hasn't always been like this. If we travelled back 1,000 years in Britain, we'd find that everyone had only a first name. Here are some Anglo-Saxon first names:

for men: Edwin, Altfrith, Osric, Cynwulf, Alfred, Cadmon, Oswald
for women: Waldgith, Edith, Frithild, Ethelfleda, Eadgifu, Elfrida, Hilda

If we wanted to distinguish between two people with the same name, we'd have to say something like 'Edwin the baker' or 'Edwin from Derby'. The idea of a proper surname developed during the Middle Ages, when people started saying things like 'Edwin Baker' or 'Edwin Derby'. That's why so many surnames are names of jobs, like these:

Potter, Smith, Cook, Taylor, Shakespeare (that is, a soldier who 'shook a spear')

or the names of the places where people came from:

Hall, Norman ('man from the north'), Street, Wood

Another way of making a surname was to describe the look of a person, or how they behaved, such as 'John Long' as opposed to 'John Short'. That's where surnames like these come from:

Black, Little, Young, Rich, Armstrong, Swift

And if a man had no obvious distinguishing features, there was an easy way out. Simply call him the 'son of' someone or the 'kin of' someone. If it's a girl, just say 'Mary (belonging to) Thomas' – so, Mary Thomas. That's where surnames like these come from:

Johnson, Robertson, Watkins, Nicholas

In Iceland, they always name people in relation to their parents. If my first name is Eric, and I have a son and a daughter, they will be called Ericsson and Ericsdottir ('Eric's daughter').

Sometimes we have to do some detective work before we can understand why people had a particular surname. Why was someone called Newman? Probably because he was a newcomer to an area. Why was someone called Palmer? Because he had made a pilgrimage to the Holy Land, carrying a palm. Why was someone called Leach? Because he was a doctor, and used leeches to treat people.

Once we have our name, we tend to stay with it all our lives. What sort of thing would make people change their name? It can happen during some types of religious ceremony. In some countries, during the Christian ceremony of Confirmation, people add a saint's name to the names they already have. Someone converting to a new religion will often change their first name – as did the boxer Cassius Clay when he became a Muslim, Muhammad Ali. And when a woman becomes a nun, in some religions she can take on a new name – even a male one. So, in Christianity, we find such names as Sister Luke or Sister Bernard – the names of famous male saints.

People also deliberately change their names when they don't like the one they have – or don't think it sounds right for the job they do. These new names are called *pseudonyms* (pronounced 'syooduh-nims'). That's why many writers, film stars, and pop stars change their names. Do you know who Charles Dodgson, Marshall Bruce Mathers, and David McDonald are? You'll know them better as author Lewis Carroll (*Alice in Wonderland*), pop star Eminem, and actor David Tennant (*Dr Who*).

Sometimes, the person doesn't have any choice. Actors can't use their real names if there's already another actor with that name. They have to change it. It would get very confusing otherwise. That's why the American film star Michael J. Fox has the 'J' in his name. And British actor David Walliams (*Little Britain*) couldn't use David Williams for the same reason.

Getting married is the most usual time that a surname changes. But there are more ways of doing this than you might think.

- The traditional method is for the wife to take her husband's surname. So, if Mary Williams marries Michael Smith, she becomes Mary Smith.
- An alternative is that the wife takes her husband's surname but continues to use her own name as a middle name. So, if Mary Williams marries Michael Smith, she becomes Mary Williams Smith. Sometimes the husband does the same thing, so he would become Michael Williams Smith. They can then join the two names with a hyphen, to make a 'double-barrelled' surname: Mary and Michael Williams-Smith.
- Another option is that the wife keeps her maiden name at work but uses her husband's name at home, so she ends up with two names. This happens a lot when the woman is a celebrity whose maiden name is well known.
- Very occasionally, a husband takes his wife's maiden name. So, if Mary Williams marries Michael Smith, he becomes Michael Williams.
- But what happens if you don't want to choose which name to keep, the man's or the woman's? Or you can't decide which name should go first if you want to keep both? There's a solution. In recent years, especially in

the USA, couples 'mesh' their name – making a new surname out of the two old ones. So, if Mary Williams marries Michael Smith they could become Mr and Mrs Willsmith or Mr and Mrs Smithiams.

We all have one first name, right? Wrong. Most people have more than one, because most of us have a pet name or a nickname. Somebody called Elizabeth might also be called Liz, Lizzy, Lisbet, Beth, Betsy, Elsie, or any of several other forms of the name. These would usually be used only by Elizabeth's family and friends. And Elizabeth might also have a nickname. If she had fair hair, she might be called Blondie, for instance.

The word 'nickname' first began to be used in the Middle Ages, where it was originally 'an eke name'. 'Eke' (pronounced 'eek') meant 'also'. A nickname was an extra name, showing a special relationship. People who are friends give each other nicknames:

Chuck for Charles
Spike for Michael
Ginger for someone with red hair
Spud for someone whose surname is Murphy (because 'spud' and 'murphy' are both slang terms for a potato)

Lovers give each other nicknames, such as Sweetypie and Mouse. Nicknames are not always nice, of course, especially when children use them. Nobody wants to be called Piggy, Porky, or Four-Eyes, but we hear that sort of thing quite a bit.

We don't choose these sorts of nickname. We're given them by others. Students give their teachers nicknames. Journalists give politicians nicknames. Criminals often have nicknames, such as Scarface Al Capone or Jack the Ripper. Even kings and queens can have nicknames, such as Richard the Lionheart (Richard I) or the Merry Monarch (Charles II).

Groups of people can have nicknames too, especially organizations in the public eye. Who are the Tories? The Conservative Party in the UK. Who are the Gunners? Arsenal football team. Do you go shopping in Marks and Sparks? Marks and Spencers. Even a city can have a nickname, or a state. What British city is called Pompey? Portsmouth. What is the Lone Star State? Texas.

But there's one situation where we do choose our nickname. That's when we're on the internet. If you join a chatgroup or a social network, such as Facebook, or send comments to blogs, or send emails, you can if you want adopt a nickname – or 'nick', as it's usually called. There are some very inventive nicks out in cyberspace. People call themselves by all sorts of crazy names.

Stardude, Crazybabe, Yoyo, Dave66, XXYYZZ

You don't even have to be able to pronounce them!

DO YOU KNOW ALF A BETT?

Writers love to make up names that reflect their characters. Charles Dickens has some splendid examples, such as Scrooge, Pecksniff, Bumble, and Sweedlepipe. J. K. Rowling has Hagrid, Kettleburn, Dumbledore, Sprout, and many more.

It's interesting how some names sound good and some sound bad. Names with soft consonants such as [m], [n], and [l] tend to sound nicer than names with hard consonants such as [k] and [g]. Imagine we're approaching a planet, where two alien races live. One of the races is called the Lamonians. The other is called the Grataks. Which sounds like the friendlier race? Most people opt for the Lamonians, because the name sounds friendlier. Grataks sound nasty.

People like to play with the sounds in names too. We find lots of names like these in joke books, and it's good fun making up new ones.

Chris Cross　　**Jim Nasium**　　**Mustapha Camel**

Dan D Lion　　**Laura Norder**　　**Noah Zark**

Dinah Mite　　**Minnie Buss**　　**Patty Cake**

Eva Brick　　**Mona Lott**　　**Stan Dupp**

CHAPTER 29

The electronic revolution

The computer has changed the nature of our language lives. For the first few years of our life, all we could do was listen and speak. At about age five, we learned to read and write. Just a few people, when they were much older, learned to type, using a typewriter. And that was it. Then along came computers and mobile phones, and now millions and millions are using keyboards and keypads to communicate with each other electronically. Even very young children. I know several three-year-olds who can find the letters of their name on a keyboard and send them onto a screen. They can't write yet, but they can type.

Typing speed is slow to start with, but it soon gets fast. And once we're fluent typists, we can do something that was never possible on the old typewriters. We can use our fingers to have a normal conversation. Look at the way this conversation flies along. Jane and Eric are instant messaging each other.

Jane: hi
Eric: hi
Jane: gotta mo?
Eric: sure
Jane: thought u might b
Jane: havin a bath

Eric: no
Eric: had one last week
Jane: ☺
Eric: or was it last month??!!
Eric: cant rememebr

That exchange took less than half a minute. It's a lot slower than if they were face-to-face and talking to each other, but it's still pretty fast.

It's easy to see, from the way they type, that Jane and Eric are young people. They're chatting in a very casual and modern way – 'hi', 'gotta', 'mo' (for 'moment') – and they spell the way they speak, leaving out the 'g' in 'havin'. They're using internet abbreviations ('u' and 'b'). Eric types 'remember' wrongly. They're not bothering to start their sentences with capital letters. They don't use standard punctuation. They leave out full stops at the ends of sentences, as well as the apostrophe in 'cant'. Eric has an unusual number of punctuation marks at one point ('??!!'), and Jane uses punctuation marks which appear on screen in the form of a smiley, or emoticon.

Some people would say that this exchange shows Jane and Eric aren't very good at English. We might hear comments like this: 'They don't know how to punctuate or use capital letters. And Eric doesn't even know how to spell "remember"! It's terrible!' Are they right?

No, they're not. I happen to know Jane and Eric. In fact, I got a letter from Jane a little while ago which started like this:

Dear David,
           Thank you very much for your message of a few days ago. I'm sorry I haven't been able to answer it until now, but I've been on holiday.

Obviously she does know how to use full stops and apostrophes. And if you read the whole of her letter, you wouldn't find a single spelling mistake. Clearly she does know how to use the standard form of the English language. And Eric is the same. In fact, Eric is a well-known author, who writes books for a living.

What Jane and Eric have done is learn a new style of writing English which is suitable for the computer. The whole point of instant messaging is that the exchanges should take place as quickly as possible. That's why it's called 'instant'. So the writers don't waste time by using extra keystrokes. It would slow things down quite a lot if they used the shift key on their keyboard to make a capital letter at the beginning of each sentence. And if a sentence is clear without a punctuation mark, then they don't bother to put one in. Similarly, they don't waste time correcting a typing error if the word is recognizable. It's obvious what 'rememebr' is, so Eric leaves it alone.

The exchange also shows some ways of using language that are brand new. Look at that emoticon. If this had been a face-to-face conversation, we can imagine how Jane would have reacted at that point. She'd have laughed. Now it's possible for her to laugh in print – by using the smiley face. It saves her having to think up some words to express her feeling. She could have written 'ha ha', or 'lol' ('laughing out loud'), or something else, but the smiley makes the point more directly.

Notice too the way Jane and Eric sometimes break their sentences up into chunks, like this:

Jane: thought u might b
Jane: havin a bath

People like to keep their turns short, when instant messaging. It's very unusual to find a chunk that's more than six or seven words. So when somebody starts a sentence that's going to go on a bit, we'll usually find that it's split into small chunks. Here's another example from later in the conversation:

Jane: i just wanted to know
Jane: if youve finished with the dvd
Jane: u borrowed last week

Jane: cos Emma would like to see it

When someone does this, of course, it allows the other person to break in with a reply at any time. If Eric guessed what Jane was about to ask, he might have done this:

Jane: i just wanted to know
Jane: if youve finished with the dvd
Eric: yes
Jane: u borrowed last week
Eric: it was great
Jane: cos Emma would like to see it

That's a very strange-looking conversation. It's not the sort of thing we'd do if we were talking face-to-face. And it certainly isn't like any kind of written conversation we've ever seen before in novels or plays. It's like two people talking at the same time. But it all makes sense, and once people get used to using the computer in this way, they don't even notice that the two strands of the chat are weaving together like this.

Instant messaging is just one of the new ways of communicating which the computer makes available to us. There are many others.

- We can send emails.
- We can join a chatroom.
- We can write a blog.
- We can join a social network, such as Facebook.
- We can send short messages, using a system such as Twitter.
- We can send text messages.
- We can search Web pages.
- We can play online games.
- We can use our computer like a telephone.

The amazing thing is that most of these possibilities are very recent. The World Wide Web wasn't invented until 1991. Most people never emailed before the mid-1990s. A search system such as Google wasn't around until 1999. Text-messaging didn't take off until the turn of the century. Blogging became popular soon after that. Facebook began in 2004. Twitter in 2006. In other words – I'm writing in 2009 – most of the things we do online have been around for only 10 years or so. Yet it feels as if they've been with us for ever.

For young people, of course, these things *have* been with them for ever. If you're in your teens, you won't remember a time when there was no internet. You've grown up with it all around you. You've learned, almost without thinking, how to talk and write on computers in a natural way, just as you did when you were learning your mother tongue. Older people haven't had it so easy. For them, learning how to communicate on computers has been more like learning a foreign language!

Actually, it would be more accurate to say 'languages'. Because one of the interesting things about the way we communicate by computer is that there are many different styles. We don't write in the same way when we email or blog or send a text. In fact the software sometimes won't allow us to do so. If we want to send a message using Twitter, it has to be less than 140 characters of our alphabet. Text-messaging allows us up to 160. That means our language is going to be very different from what we do when we write a blog, where there's no such limitation, or send a message to a Facebook forum.

To see how distinctive electronic language can be, the next chapter will take a closer look at one of the most popular mediums, text-messaging.

DON'T SHOUT

What would you think if you got an email message like this?

WILL YOU BRING MY DVD ROUND PLEASE. TED

It might give you a bit of a fright, because it's all in capital letters. It's as if Ted is shouting at you. Is he upset? Is he cross?

In fact, all that's probably happened is that Ted left the caps lock key on by mistake, so that everything came out in capital letters. And he didn't think of the effect that this might have on you.

It's bad 'netiquette' to shout in this way. It's also harder to read. Computer style manuals say DON'T do it – unless you really mean to.

Capitalizing the occasional word, by way of emphasis, is all right, of course. There's nothing wrong with typing this:

I thought the film was GREAT.

But you'll see other ways of emphasizing a word, such as changing the typeface or adding spaces, asterisks, or underbars.

I thought the film was **great.**
I thought the film was g r e a t.
I thought the film was *great*.
I thought the film was _great_.

It's too early to say which of these methods will become the standard way of showing emphasis. People will vote by using their fingers. (I use the asterisk one, myself.)

CHAPTER 30

Texting

'It's a crazy new language. I can't understand a word of it!' That's what I once heard someone say about text-messaging. And the speaker went on: 'If it carries on like this, the young people of today will end up not knowing how to spell!'

Well, you readers are the kind of young people this person was thinking of. Is it true? You probably all text. Is 'textese' really a new language? And do you really not know how to spell?

As soon as we start to study texts carefully, as a good linguist should, it turns out that they aren't as weird as some people believe. Here are some examples of real texts that I've collected.

> u 2. Glad journey went OK.
> what r u saying?
> Landed safely. On way to town. xxx
> i'll b there by 7
> we've just had a drink with Jon!!!!

Who sent these texts? All sorts of people. The first and last ones were from teenagers. The others were from people in their 40s and 50s.

Here are two more examples. Who sent these, do you think?

Tropical Storm Barry (Atlantic) has formed, located 320 miles (520 km) Southwest of Tampa Florida.

Barack has chosen Senator Joe Biden to be our VP nominee.

The first was from an American weather station, alerting people to an approaching storm. The second was from the campaign office of Barack Obama, in August 2008, when he announced who his vice-president was going to be. Notice that, in these messages, there are none of the abbreviations we associate with texting. They're in standard English spelling, with proper use of capital letters and punctuation marks.

Most of the text messages flying around the world right now are like these. They're being sent by organizations such as radio and TV stations, schools and colleges, shops and businesses, religious groups, and government bodies. The messages are sending information about what's going on in the world, and asking us for our reactions. We hardly ever see abbreviations in them like 'c u l8r'. Indeed, most organizations don't allow their texters to use them, because they know there's a risk that the people receiving the texts won't understand them.

Even the texts sent by teenagers aren't as strange as some people make them out to be. Here's a research task that anyone can do. We make a collection of texts, and count up all the words in them. Next, we count just the words which are 'textisms' – abbreviations like 'c', 'l8r', 'msg', and so on. What result will we get? Let's try it on these two birthday texts sent by teenagers:

happy birthday 2 u. hope this day is the best and all ur wishes come true. love and kisses from me and tom

hey 1 year older now. does that mean a yr smarter? have a gr8 day. light the candles. cut the cake. dance and shake. luv from all @ the club

Text abbreviations		*Normal words*		
u	happy	wishes	older	candles
2	birthday	come	now	cut
ur	hope	true	does	cake
yr	this	love	that	dance
gr8	day	kisses	mean	shake
luv	is	from (x2)	smarter	club
@	the (x4)	me	have	all (x2)
1	best	tom	a (x2)	year
	and (x4)	hey	day	light

TOTAL 8   45

This is a typical result. Only a small proportion of the words in a collection of texts are actually textisms. Usually it's somewhere between 10 and 20 per cent. Most people find that surprising.

Another surprise comes when people learn that the so-called 'new' abbreviations aren't new at all. Have such forms as 'u' for 'you' and 'gr8' for 'great' been created just for mobile phones? Not at all. We can find people using those kinds of abbreviations over 200 years ago. They were called *rebuses* (pronounced 'ree-buses'), and they were a very popular kind of puzzle. Queen Victoria used to play rebus games. So did Lewis Carroll.

When I was a boy, I used to get Christmas annuals which had rebus games. They were a bit like the way some early writing systems developed, as we saw in Chapter 17. I would see a row of symbols like this, and would have to work out what they were saying:

YY U R YY U B I C U R YY 4 ME

Most adults will remember that one. It reads:

too wise you are, too wise you be, I see you are too wise for me

So anyone who thinks that textese is a 'new language' is wrong.

Almost all the abbreviations commonly seen in English texts have been in the language for years. And the same applies to other languages. Very few are brand new: 'lol', for 'laughing out loud', is a new one; so is 'brb' – 'be right back'.

Of course, young texters play games with abbreviations, just as their grandparents did. They love to make up new ones, and the crazier the better. Here are some I've seen:

imo	in my opinion
imho	in my humble opinion
imnsho	in my not so humble opinion
imhbco	in my humble but correct opinion
rotfl	rolling on the floor laughing
rotflol	rolling on the floor laughing out loud
rotfluts	rolling on the floor laughing unable to speak
rotflmao	rolling on the floor laughing my ass off

People have actually made dictionaries listing hundreds of creations like this. But hardly any of these turn up in the texts people send to each other day by day.

Why did people start using abbreviations when they began to send text messages? The obvious reason is that it saves time and energy. It's much quicker to type 'u' than 'you'. We also see that sort of abbreviation used in other areas of computer communication where people want to type quickly, such as chatrooms and emails.

However, there's a second reason. People thought it was good fun. They thought it was cool to send messages which played around with spellings – leaving letters out and using symbols to replace letters, such as '8' and '@'. This was something they couldn't do in other kinds of writing.

But think about it. As I said in Chapter 9, if it's cool to leave letters out, we have to know they're there in the first place. In other words, we have to know how to spell before we can text well. And we have to know how to relate letters to sounds, otherwise we're never going to be able to write 'gr8' and '2day'. It should come as no surprise, then, to learn that the best texters are the best spellers.

If we're really good at texting, we'll probably be quite creative too. The evidence is in the way people play with text language and write text-message poems. They also try to translate the titles of famous books or films into textese, like this:

ChRlE & t chocl8 factrE
Alice in 1derl&

And several text poetry competitions have now been held. I think some of the poems are brilliant. This is one of my favourites, sent to a school competition for 5- to 12-year-olds in Australia a few years ago:

quik hurry up & txt me
tell me u luv me
tell me how much u want me
tell me im da 1
oops wrong prsn
i sent it 2 my mum

It's a challenge, writing a poem with a limit of 160 characters and making the lines fit nicely into the phone's screen. You don't have to use abbreviations, if you don't want to, and some of the most effective poems are entirely in Standard English spelling. Here's one that was written for a BBC television programme in 2005 about the accents and dialects heard in Wales:

This is my voice
The voice of my family
The voice of my friends
The voice of my town
The voice of my past
The voice of my future
The voice of my heart
This is one of the voices of Wales

That's 144 characters, without spaces.

This isn't the first time that poets have tried to write within very strict limits, of course. The *haiku* (pronounced 'high-coo') is a famous example, which has been written in Japan for hundreds of years. It's a very short poem, capturing a moment of experience, which usually has no more than 17 syllables and no more than three lines. It's possible to adapt the style to English. Here's an example:

sunflash of sea birds
flying beyond the horizon
time to move on

So let's do that.

TEXTING ABROAD

How do people text in other languages? The answer is: in the same sort of way that we do in English. They leave out letters and they make numbers replace sounds.

The French word for 'thank you' is 'merci', pronounced 'mare-see'. The French word for 'six' looks like the English word, but is pronounced differently, often as 'see'. So French texters often write 'merci' as 'mr6'.

The German word for 'attention' is 'achtung'. The German word for 'eight' is 'acht'. So German texters often write 'achtung' as '8ung'.

The Spanish word for 'greetings' is 'saludos', pronounced 'sa-loo-doss'. The Spanish word for 'two' is 'dos', also pronounced 'doss'. So Spanish texters often write 'saludos' as 'salu2'.

The Welsh word for 'now' is 'nawr', pronounced like the English word but with an 'r' at the end. The Welsh word for 'nine' is 'naw', pronounced 'now'. So Welsh texters often write 'nawr' as '9r'.

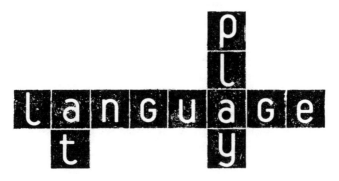

CHAPTER 31

Language at play

Texting shows how quickly people are ready to play with language. Very soon after the mobile phone was invented, they started to send texts to each other which played with the normal spellings of words. Not long after that, as we saw in Chapter 30, they started texting poetry. And not just poetry. In some parts of the world, such as China and Japan, millions of people receive daily instalments of the latest text-message novels!

We love to play with language, and we enjoy it when other people play with language. And we're playful in hundreds of different ways. Every area of language that we've discussed in this book can be used for fun, but people especially like playing with sounds and letters.

Every day we hear someone putting on a funny voice. It might be Homer Simpson, or Ali G, or Bugs Bunny, or any of dozens of characters we know from films and television. A student might imitate the voice of a teacher. A boy might make fun of the voice of a girl in the same class – or the other way round. Someone might suddenly put on an American voice (if they're British) or a British voice (if they're American), or a 'country yokel' voice or a 'pirate' voice, and go around saying 'ooh-arr'. Everyone can do silly voices, and some people are absolutely brilliant at them. They'll probably become actors or TV impressionists one day.

Another popular way of playing with sounds is to make puns.

A pun happens when we take a word that has one meaning and replace it by another word sounding the same but with a different meaning. Here's an example:

> You shouldn't write with a broken pencil because it's pointless.

The word 'point' has two meanings: 'sharp end' and 'purpose'. We have to know both meanings before we get the joke, of course.

Sometimes the words involved in the pun don't have exactly the same sounds, but they're close enough for us to make the connection.

> Patient: Doctor, doctor, I think I'm a bird.
> Doctor: I'll tweet you in a minute.

This is quite a clever pun, because we have to know (1) that birds go 'tweet', (2) that doctors 'treat' patients, and (3) that people sometimes say a 'w' sound instead of an 'r' – such as the British TV personality, Jonathan Ross.

Birthday cards often pile on pun after pun after pun. If we love cats, someone might decide to send a card like this:

> I didn't FUR-get
> I looked in the CATalogue
> And found this card.
> So do PAWS
> And have a PURR-fect birthday

People also love to play games with the letters of the alphabet. Scrabble is probably the best-known example, building words out of letter tiles to see who can get the highest score. But there are lots of letter games we can play by ourselves.

- Make words or sentences which read the same way in both directions:

Was it a cat I saw? Madam, I'm Adam.

These are called *palindromes*.

- Make words where the letters are changed around to make a new word with a related meaning:

    the eyes = they see. Harry Potter = try trap hero

    These are called *anagrams*.

- Make sentences where no use is made of a particular letter, such as 'e', the most frequent letter in the English alphabet:

    I am going to show you how to do this right now.

    These are called *lipograms*. An author called Ernest Wright once wrote a novel called *Gadsby* which was 50,000 words long, and didn't have a single letter 'e' inside it.

- Make sentences where every word contains the same vowel:

    Cool schoolboys do not do sports on top of London shopfronts.

    These are called *univocalics*, pronounced 'you-nee-voh-cal-iks'.

Comics and Christmas annuals contain many other examples, such as crossword puzzles, or letter-squares containing hidden words. It's easy to make up your own games in this way. Try composing a sentence in which every word starts with a letter of the alphabet – in the right order! Here's one:

A big cowboy, dancing elegantly for grand hotels in Jersey, knitting lovely mittens nicely on pretty quilted rubber shoes, thought untrained vets would X-ray yellow zebras.

I didn't say it had to make sense!

One of the best places to study language at play is right under your noses: in a school playground, especially in a primary school. There we'll see all kinds of games taking place in which the activities are being controlled by the language. Watch some children skipping, or bouncing a ball, or counting out partners in a game, and we'll see they do it in time to language. We'll hear rhymes like these:

> I like coffee,
> I like tea,
> I like radio
> And TV.

> One, two, three,
> Mother caught a flea,
> Put it in the teapot
> And made a cup of tea.
> The flea jumped out,
> Mother gave a shout,
> In came father
> With his shirt hanging out.

We'll also hear lots of nonsense games, or games which get one of the players into trouble.

> One fine day in the middle of the night,
> Two dead men got up to fight,
> Back to back they faced each other
> Drew their swords and shot each other.

> Silence in the courtyard,
> Silence in the street,
> The biggest twit in England
> Is just about to speak – starting from now!

Scholars have made collections of these rhymes. There are thousands of them. Each generation uses some of the old ones, and makes up new ones.

Why does everybody play with language like this? We tell riddles, make up rhymes, talk backwards, make up tongue-twisters, pretend to talk in foreign languages, and tell all kinds of jokes – 'knock-knock' jokes, 'elephant' jokes, 'doctor-doctor' jokes, and thousands more. Yes, thousands. I have a book called *A Thousand Jokes for Kids*. Most of the jokes are so bad they make you groan. But then, that's part of the fun.

Why do we do all this? I gave a hint of the answer in the very first chapter of this book. Do you remember I began by saying 'We sometimes do some silly things with language'? And I went on to talk about how, when a baby is born, we talk to it using baby-talk? Well, baby-talk is language play. That's what we hear, from the moment we're born. The people around us are always playing with language. No wonder we grow up wanting to do it as well.

As babies get older, the language play becomes more varied. When they're about six months of age, parents play such games as 'peep-bo' and 'round-and-round-the-garden'. In the second year of life, they start hearing simple nursery rhymes and songs. They play bouncing games, such as 'The Grand Old Duke of York'. Story-time introduces them to a world of colourful characters, such as giants and pigs and wolves, who talk in strange ways. TV and DVDs introduce them to Mickey Mouse, Goofy, Donald Duck (now there's a really weird use of language!), Tigger, Pooh, and a host of cartoon characters, most of whom have crazy voices. By the time they get to school age, children must feel that life is largely a language playground.

When they start school, of course, they learn the sad truth! Language isn't just for fun. It's there for serious purposes too.

GRAFFITI RULES, OK?

We don't just hear language play all around us. We see it, too, in the form of graffiti. Now, I don't like the way people mess things up by writing all over them, but I have to admit that graffiti do sometimes show some very clever kinds of language play. The 'OK' theme is a good example.

Nobody knows exactly when people started writing that something 'rules, OK?' on walls. It was probably in the early 1900s, and the most likely explanation is that it all started with rival gangs each boasting that they ruled – that is, they were the best. But football team supporters were there too:

ARSENAL RULES, OK?

The formula has since been taken over and used in thousands of different ways. It's easy enough to make your own collection, but there are several books which have brought together hundreds of the best examples. Here are some of my favourites:

James Bond rules, OOK?

Queen Elizabeth rules UK

Sausage rolls, OK?

And, of course:

Grammar rules, OK?

CHAPTER 32

Why use language?

What's it all for? Why did the human race learn to speak, write, and sign? What's the use of language? We might think the answer is very simple: to communicate with each other. That's how I talked about it earlier in the book. But there's more to it than that.

Certainly the primary purpose of language is for communication. We use language to communicate our ideas and opinions to each other. We use it to ask other people for information and to tell them our thoughts when they ask us. Sometimes we tell the truth. Sometimes we tell lies. But in all these cases, the basic aim is clear. We want the ideas in our head to get into someone else's head. And for that to happen we must speak them, write them, or sign them.

But there are several other uses of language where the basic aim is nothing to do with communicating ideas. I've just been talking about one of these in Chapter 31: being playful.

Imagine a group of people swopping puns. Mary starts it off by telling the others that her cat hasn't been well, and this leads John to say:

Aw, poor thing, did it have catarrh?

Everybody laughs, and then they produce as many 'cat' puns as they can think of:

> What a catastrophe!
> A catalogue of disasters!
> She must have been eating caterpillars.
> Perhaps she got her paws caught in her catapult.

The cat doesn't understand a word of what they're saying, but everyone else is having a great time, groaning away as the puns get worse and worse.

Let's pause now and think about this kind of language. It isn't language being used for communicating ideas. The cat didn't have catarrh. She hadn't been eating caterpillars. She didn't have a catapult. This is language being used to talk nonsense – and nobody minds at all, because it's fun.

Here's another use of language which has nothing to do with communicating ideas: to express identity. Earlier in the book, in Chapter 12, I talked about accents and dialects. These tell people who we are and where we come from. They are one way in which we express our identities.

There are other ways. Listen to the chanting of a crowd at a football match.

COME ON YOU ROYALS! COME ON YOU ROYALS!

They might say this hundreds of times during the match. There are no 'ideas', as such, being communicated here. The people are chanting to show support for their team. Their chant shows whose side they are on. It expresses their identity.

Identity can be expressed in writing too. Next time you go into a newspaper shop, notice how the different papers identify themselves. Some, such as the *Sun* and the *Mirror* in the UK, stand out because they have big red banners at the top of the front page. And each paper has its own distinctive typeface. We can easily spot *The New York Times*, for instance:

The New York Times

No other newspaper in the USA uses a typeface quite like that.

Another use of language is to express our emotions. Imagine you're hammering a nail into a piece of wood, but something goes wrong and you hit your finger instead. What will come out of your mouth? Of course, if you're very brave you might not say anything. But most of us would let out a yell. And quite a few people would shout at the hammer. 'Stupid hammer!' we might moan, as if it was the hammer's fault. And rather a large number of people, I suspect, would swear out loud, and say 'bloody hell' – or something much worse.

What sort of language is this? If we call the hammer stupid, it can hardly be the communication of ideas, can it? The hammer doesn't have a brain, so it can't possibly understand us. So what are we doing, talking to the hammer?

What we're doing is getting rid of our nervous energy. By shouting at the hammer, we feel a bit better. That's why we might swear at it. It makes us feel better. Everyone swears, even if their strong words are very mild, such as 'Gosh!' or 'Sugar!' or 'Crikey!'

This emotional use of language can actually be useful in another way. By sounding off, we let other people know that something has gone wrong. The swear words are actually a cry for help. So this kind of language does communicate information of a sort, but it isn't very clear information, as we can see from this dialogue:

John (banging his thumb): Ow! Stupid hammer!
Mum: What's the matter?
John: I've banged my thumb!

John's first utterance doesn't say very much really. It's the follow-up utterance that tells Mum what's happened. John is using language in two very different ways.

We also use language just to get on with other people. Think of what happens when we sneeze. Usually, in English, someone says 'Bless you!' And the sneezer then says 'Thank you'. Why do we do that?

This is another use of language – to avoid embarrassment. When we make an unexpected noise, such as a sneeze, we feel a bit awkward. We can't just say nothing. That would be an awkward silence. So either *we* have to say something or the people around us have to say something. And usually it's the listeners who jump in first.

There are many occasions when we say something just to fill an otherwise awkward silence. This is why people sometimes say such things as 'Looks like rain' or 'Lovely day' when they meet each other. They don't want to start a proper conversation, but they feel it would be rude to pass by in silence. So they make a remark about the weather.

The same sort of thing happens when I meet people for the first time, and they say 'How do you do?' They're not actually asking me how I am. There's no request for information here. They'd be very surprised if I started to tell them all about my health: 'Thank you for asking. Actually, I've got a bit of a temperature today, and I think I've got a cold coming on. And I had a bit of a tummy upset last night.' No, all they expect is for me to say 'How do you do?' back to them. It's just a greeting.

Every day, we show how we're getting on with other people by using language to build social relationships. That's why we say such things as 'Hi', 'Good night', and 'See you later'. It shows that we're getting on well with the people we're talking to. And if we don't say such things, it shows the opposite.

We can also use language to change the world! Imagine the scene. A ship is being launched at a shipyard, and the Queen of England is there to name it. A bottle of champagne is attached to the end of a rope. After she says 'I name this ship… ', the rope swings, the bottle breaks on the ship's hull, and the ship slides into the water for the first time.

This is a very unusual use of language. We're using it to change how we see the world. Before the Queen spoke, the ship didn't officially have a name. After she spoke, it did. It was the language that made the difference.

The same sort of thing happens in a number of other situations. Have you ever been to an auction? The auctioneer is selling an object, and the people who want to buy it make their bids. When the auctioneer sees that the bidding is over, he calls out:

GOING … GOING … GONE

As soon as he says the word 'Gone', and bangs his hammer – and not before – the object is sold. Again, it is the language that makes the difference.

Many religions and societies have ceremonies which people have to go through if they want to join. Christians have to be baptized, and the person doesn't become a Christian until the words 'I baptize thee … ' have been spoken by the minister who is carrying out the baptism. In religions all over the globe, people believe they are changing lives when they pray for help, give blessings, and carry out other spiritual tasks. Similarly, in some societies, magic rituals are thought to affect the nature of the world. In all cases, the rituals rely on language.

Magic sounds a bit far out. But think about it. We don't promise anything until we say the words 'I promise'. We don't apologize until we say 'I'm sorry'. That's magical too.

I've left until last one of the most important uses of language: we use it to help us think. Have you ever talked to yourself? It can sometimes be very helpful when you're on your own and trying to work out a problem. I once overheard someone building a piece of equipment in which there were all sorts of coloured wires and screws and things. He was looking first at the instructions, then at what he was doing, and all the time he was talking to himself like this:

Right, so the green wire goes to the left-hand screw and the

red wire goes to the middle one. Right … Good … That leaves
the blue and orange ones which go …

He paused, looked at the instructions again, then went on:

… the blue to the middle one as well … no, that can't be
right …

and he carried on talking like this until the job was done.

Why was he talking? He wasn't talking to me (I was outside the
room) and there was nobody else around. Plainly, it helped him to
think. By saying the instructions out loud, he was making it easier
to remember what to do.

We all do similar things, when we try to remember instructions.
That's why we sometimes repeat what someone else has said:

Mary: So take the first left, then the second right, go through
a set of traffic lights, and John's road is the first on the left.
Me: So, first left, second right, through the lights, first on
left.
Mary: That's right.
Me (muttering, as I start my journey): First left, second right,
through the lights, first on left … first left, second right …

We do the same sort of thing in our writing, when we make notes to
help us organize our thoughts on a page, or when we make a rough
draft of something. The very act of writing something down, or
putting it on a screen, can help us work out what it is we're trying
to say. Authors sometimes make hundreds of drafts before they're
happy that what they've written is what they want to say. As we'll
see in Chapter 35, this happens especially in literature, which is
another very special use of language. And one of the reasons is that
words don't just express meanings; they express feelings too.

LANGUAGE FOR LINKING

The internet has introduced us to a new use of language: the hypertext link. This is the piece of text that we click on when we want to move from one page to another or from one site to another. It's usually coloured or underlined in a special way. It might be a full web address (such as 'www.davidcrystal.com'), a heading of some sort (such as 'News' or 'Shopping Basket'), or just a word (such as 'click here').

It now seems so natural to click on these links that we fail to notice what a novel use of language this is. This is language whose sole purpose is to get you from A to B. Was there ever anything like it in written language before the internet came along?

The nearest thing was the use of footnotes and cross-references. If I see this in a book:

The animals live in special cages.[1]

the numeral tells me that there is a similarly numbered note somewhere which will give me some extra information. It might be at the foot of the page or at the back of the book. This is a bit like a hypertext link – except that we can't click on it! Similarly, if we saw this:

The animals live in separate cages (see p. 318).

the cross-reference is a bit like a hypertext link too.

But there's a huge difference between these features and hypertext links. We don't *have to* use footnotes or cross-references in traditional written language. Many publications don't have them at all. But if there were no hypertext links there wouldn't be an internet. That's why the system is called an 'interNET' and why the World Wide Web is called a 'WEB'. It's a way of sharing the information contained in all the computers in the world linked by the same connecting system (or 'protocol'). And language is the means that makes it all happen.

CHAPTER 33

Language for feelings

Language often allows us several ways of saying the same thing, but there's a very slight difference between them. Here are Mary, Susan, and Joan talking about some children playing in the next room.

Mary: Listen to those little ones!
Susan: Listen to those urchins!
Joan: Listen to those brats!

The words tell us something about the feelings of the speakers. Mary must think the kids are really sweet. Susan must think they're being a bit of a mischief, and probably they're not very well dressed. And Joan must think they're being a real pain. If they didn't want to show their feelings, of course, they could just say: 'Listen to those children.' 'Children' is a neutral word.

The feelings we have when we see or hear a word are called *connotations*. 'Little ones', 'urchins', and 'brats' have different connotations. Some connotations are *positive* – they give us pleasant or comfortable feelings. Some connotations are *negative* – they give us unpleasant or uncomfortable feelings.

Every language has hundreds of words which make us think of things in an emotional way. Here are some more word-pairs which mean the same thing. In each case, I've put the 'good' meaning first and the 'bad' meaning second.

Joanne is very slim.
Joanne is very skinny.

Our house is cosy.
Our house is cramped.

He was behaving in a childlike way.
He was behaving in a childish way.

The cakes I've made are moist.
The cakes I've made are soggy.

A few more? We don't approve of people who are 'miserly', 'stingy', and 'nitpicking'. We do approve of them if they're 'thrifty', 'economical', and 'meticulous'.

This is why we have to be *very* careful when we read the papers, listen to the news, or call up a website. We should always be on our guard. Are the writers trying to put their own emotions into our heads? We might see this headline in one newspaper:

TERRORISTS MOVE SOUTH

But in another, talking about the *same* group of people, we might read:

FREEDOM FIGHTERS MOVE SOUTH

We can guess, from their choice of words, which side each newpaper is on.

Or imagine a news story about a number of people who moved into an empty building because they had nowhere else to live. If it went like this:

Several vagrants now live in the building

the writer is making us think badly of their actions, because 'vagrants' has negative connotations. But if it went like this:

Several homeless people now live in the building

the writer is making us think well of them, because 'homeless' has positive connotations. It's more likely to make us feel sympathetic.

When language tries to make us think in one way rather than another, we say that it is 'biased'. Take a situation where an airport wants to build a new runway. If writers want to persuade us to support the idea, they'll write such things as 'Building a new runway will create hundreds of jobs'. If they want us to oppose the idea, they'll write such things as 'Hundreds of homes will be demolished if the runway goes ahead'. A balanced report tells both sides of a story. A biased report tells us only one side.

One of the most important reasons for finding out about language – and for reading a book like this one – is to make ourselves aware of the way people often try to manipulate our thoughts and feelings by the way they speak and write. They're trying to persuade us to behave in a certain way, and they do this by cleverly choosing certain words, sounds, and sentence patterns. We hear politicians do it, when they make a speech asking us to vote for them. We see advertisers doing it, when we see a commercial that asks us to buy something. We need to know what people are up to, so that we're not fooled. In a word, we have to understand their *rhetoric* (pronounced 'ret-o-rik').

Rhetoric is the use of language to persuade or influence people. Advertisements use lots of rhetorical features, because they're trying to persuade us to buy things. There will be words which make a product sound really attractive:

new, wonderful, beautiful, best, great value, delicious, special, extra, lovely, crunchy, safe.

You won't see ads which use words saying that the product is

smelly, dangerous, expensive, tasteless, ordinary, worst, out-of-date.

We can be sure that an ad for some sort of diet food is going to say:

This is the easy way to stay slim!

and not:

This is the easy way to stay skinny!

Ads also use clever sounds and rhythms to make the name of the product stay in our mind:

Maybe it's Maybelline! (for a brand of make-up)
You can't get better than a Kwik-Fit fitter. (for a car-parts service)

Every bit of the language in an ad is very carefully chosen so that it has the right rhetorical effect on the listener or reader. The people who write ads can take months before they get the words exactly right. And when they do get it right, the evidence is that people remember the name of the product and want to buy it.

It's not just journalists, advertisers, and politicians who use rhetoric. Everybody does. For example, Kate wants to go to a concert, but her best friend Sue doesn't. What will Kate do? She'll do her best to persuade Sue to go by talking about how good it's going to be, how it's not very expensive, and so on. That's rhetoric.

Young people hear rhetoric from their parents and teachers from a very early age. Why some food is good for them and other food isn't. Why they have to wear school uniform. Why they shouldn't beat up their little brother or sister. And parents and teachers get lots of rhetoric in return. 'Please can I go to the party. Everyone's going to be there. I won't be back late. PLEEEASE!'

In all these examples, language is not just 'communicating ideas'. It's trying to make people feel or think about ideas in a particular way. Why do we say 'please'? It's not just a matter of being polite. Saying 'please' can actually persuade people to do what we want. 'You know how to get round me,' people sometimes say. That shows the rhetoric has worked well.

We hear language being used to express feelings every time we listen to two people having an argument. Watch an episode of some TV soaps, and you'll hardly hear anything else! The characters seem to be always arguing. And as the arguments get more and more intense, the language becomes more and more emotional. People start calling each other names. They swear at each other (though there are limits to what's allowed on television). And when they can't think of anything more to say, they stop using language completely. One of them walks out in a huff and slams the door. The argument is over – but only for the time being. The characters will have to talk to each other again in the next episode.

It's difficult to keep our feelings under control when we're having an argument. That's why it's great to do some debating. In a debate, the two sides have to present their points of view in as calm and reasoned a manner as possible and to listen to each other respectfully. It's a skill which everyone can learn. Good debaters learn how to present both sides of an argument without letting their feelings get in the way. They don't need to shout, or swear, or call names, or walk out in a huff. They let well-chosen language do all the work.

Choosing the right sort of language is certainly what we need to aim for, whenever we speak or write or sign. But that isn't always easy, as we'll see in Chapter 34.

VOTE FOR ME!

Some people are brilliant at using rhetoric to get others to support them. We can tell because of the way their listeners react. Politicians who are good speakers know how to control an audience to guarantee that they'll get a huge burst of applause. One of their tricks is to 'talk in threes', like this, with each sentence getting louder:

I don't just MAKE promises, like the opposition does.
And I don't BREAK promises, like the opposition does.
I KEEP my promises. (CHEERS)

Here's Barack Obama doing the same sort of thing, within a single sentence, during his victory speech in November 2008:

It's been a long time coming, but tonight, because of what we did on this day, in this election, at this defining moment, change has come to America.

If we lay the sentence out like this, we can see the rhetoric more clearly:

It's been a long time coming, but tonight, because of what we did
    on this day,
    in this election,
    at this defining moment,
change has come to America.

The crowd went wild.

CHAPTER 34

Political correctness

In recent years, the way we describe people has changed a lot. Not so long ago, many jobs had two names, depending on whether they were done by a man or a woman.

Man's job	*Woman's job*
steward	stewardess
manager	manageress
poet	poetess
sculptor	sculptress
policeman	policewoman

These days, most of the '-ess' names have disappeared, as a result of a huge social movement to make men and women equal in the workplace. We'll still often hear 'actress', 'waitress', and a few others, but it's a long time since I've heard female poets and sculptors called 'poetesses' and 'sculptresses'. They're just plain 'poets' and 'sculptors' now. In shops female managers today are simply 'managers', on aeroplanes the cabin crew are 'flight attendants', and in police stations we find only 'police officers'.

We especially avoid using certain names if they're felt to be insulting. And if people are heard using those names, they can get into trouble – even if they didn't intend to be insulting at all.

That's what happened to Prince Harry in 2009, when a home-made video became public in which he referred to a fellow soldier from Pakistan as a 'Paki'. He was widely criticized, even though he was using the word in a friendly way, and his Pakistani colleague wasn't offended.

There are some words which have been used so insultingly in the past that it's no longer possible to use them without causing huge offence to many people. In Britain, 'Paki' is one of them. If you're an immigrant from Pakistan and you've spent your whole life hearing people call you 'Paki' in a horrible way, it's obvious that you're never going to like the word. And you're very likely going to feel upset whenever you hear it – even if it's being used as a joke by a prince.

Most people know the old rhyme:

Sticks and stones will break my bones
But names will never hurt me.

That just isn't true! Don't believe a word of it. Names do hurt. And the hurt lasts a long time. At least if someone hits us with a stone, and we get a bruise, we know that the bruise will only last a few days. But if someone hits us with a horrid name, sometimes we never forget it.

People who come to a country from another part of the world are especially likely to be called rude names. But it isn't just a racial matter. People who are different in *any* way from most others in society are going to be called rude names. Kids who wear glasses are called 'four eyes'. People without hair are called 'baldy'. And it's a sad fact of life that our society contains people who are ready to poke fun at those who are blind or deaf, or who stammer, or who have marks on their skin, or who display any medical condition that makes them different from other people. Often, the name-callers don't realize that the names they use are so hurtful. That's another good reason for reading a book on language. It helps us understand the harm people do when they call each other names.

If there are cruel names for people, which we'd like to avoid, what do we put in their place? It can actually be difficult finding a new name that everyone likes. For example, how do we talk about people who have to use wheelchairs in a way that doesn't upset them? Until not so long ago, they were still being called 'cripples', which was a name that none of them liked. The search went on for a better name. For a while, 'handicapped' and 'disabled' were popular, but there was a problem with those names too. If we call people 'handicapped' or 'disabled', it can sound as if we're saying that they can't do anything useful at all. In fact we know very well that people in wheelchairs can do fantastic things, such as play basketball and finish marathons.

You can see the problem. Is there a word in the English language which describes the fact that people are in wheelchairs without suggesting any negative connotations? The sad fact is that there isn't one. And society is still struggling to find the best way of describing people who have lost their ability to walk, or who have lost a leg or an arm. Every now and then somebody suggests a new label. We'll hear them described as 'differently abled' or 'physically challenged', for instance. None of the new ways satisfies everyone. Some like 'physically challenged'. Some hate it. If we go and ask the people who have lost their limbs, it's the same. Some are very happy to be called 'disabled'. Some hate it.

We find the same sort of problem when we try to talk about other groups of people. What should we call old people? The 'aged', the 'elderly', 'senior citizens', or something else? What should we call people with very low intelligence? 'Mentally handicapped', 're-tarded', 'intellectually challenged', 'people with learning difficulties', or something else? What should we call people who are fat? 'Over-weight', 'differently sized', 'plus-sized', or something else? Shops that sell clothes have real problems here.

In the USA people worried for years about how best to describe black people. The word 'negro' was felt to be offensive, as was a phrase like 'the blacks'. Eventually the name 'African American' became popular, and 'Afro-American' is also widespread now. But there's no guarantee that today's popular name will still be here in 10 years' time.

Governments, employers, and other social groups sometimes try to sort out the problem by favouring one name and banning another. 'That's the name everyone should use', they say. And if we don't use it, we can get into trouble. We might be fined or lose our job if we don't use the 'correct' names. This is why we see the phrase 'politically correct' used so much these days. To say that a name is politically correct (or 'PC', for short) means that it's the official name for something. It also means that this name is supposed to give no offence to the people it refers to.

The original idea behind political correctness was very good. It's great to try to avoid using language that will offend people. And by focusing on the language we use every day, it makes us think about what we're saying. It also helps us see people as they are – as whole individuals. John might go around in a wheelchair, but why should that particular thing make us talk about him as if that was his whole story? John might be brilliant at poetry or painting or a thousand other things. And I can easily imagine John being upset if the only way he hears people talking about him is by calling him 'disabled'.

Political correctness was a good idea to start with. But unfortunately, people started imagining that they were offending someone when in fact they weren't. And some went out of their way to avoid using words which actually weren't offensive at all. They were so scared they might be criticized that they invented ways of talking which were so bizarre that people just laughed at them. It still happens today. We hear comedians joking about people with false teeth being 'dentally challenged'. Or we hear the fairy tale becoming 'Snow White and the Seven Vertically Challenged Men', in case dwarfs felt it was somehow getting at them.

Many people think that the PC movement has gone too far in making us sensitive to words that are in fact quite innocent. When the word 'black' (meaning a person with black skin) was first thought to be insulting, many stories came out of the USA about people who tried to avoid using it in any circumstances. They were scared of asking for a 'black coffee', so they asked for 'coffee without milk' instead. Teachers were scared to talk about 'blackboards'. And some nursery schools – in Britain as well as the USA – went so far as to suggest that 'Baa, baa, black sheep, have you any wool?' should be replaced by 'white sheep' or even 'rainbow sheep'. Every now and then we read about such things in the papers. The proposals often cause a row, because many people think they're ridiculous.

And now I get greetings cards at Christmas which say 'Happy Holidays', not 'Happy Christmas'. I imagine the senders chose them because they were worried I might be offended if I received a card celebrating a Christian festival. That's a real shame. I know people who belong to all sorts of religions – Christians, Hindus, Jews, Muslims – and who send each other greetings cards when the time comes to celebrate their different festivals. They delight in the diversity. I know people with no religious background at all who are just as delighted to send or receive a card at a festival time. That's how it should be, to my mind. I hope the day never comes when all the cards say only 'Happy Holidays'.

Whether that happens or not won't be up to me. It's up to the next generation to decide whether political correctness has gone too far. That means you.

PC ABROAD

All the examples in Chapter 34 are from English. The English language has been a special focus of attention, because much of the concern that started the PC movement, back in the 1960s and 1970s, came from the USA.

But other languages have their PC words too. Here are three examples:

- In much the same way as a 'binman' in Britain came to be called a 'refuse collector' or 'refuse disposal officer', in Italy a 'netturbino' became an 'operatore ecologico' (or 'ecological operator').

- In France, there has been debate over the word 'aveugle' for a blind person, with the PC alternative being 'non-voyant' ('non-seeing').

- In Germany, people avoid using words which remind them of the Nazi regime of the 1930s and 1940s. In those days, the German Parliament was called the 'Reichstag' (meaning 'imperial congress'). Today, it's called the 'Bundestag' (meaning 'federal congress').

CHAPTER 35

Language in literature

Language, as we saw in Chapters 32 and 33, can make us think and make us feel. It can appeal to our head and also to our heart. And, within our heads, it can appeal to our ears and also to our eyes, by sounding or looking beautiful or ugly. Sometimes it does all four things at once. We can read something which tells us a good story, makes us laugh and cry, is nicely laid out on the page, and (when we read it aloud) is great to listen to. Language like this is most often found in novels, short stories, essays, plays, and poems. In a word, in *literature*.

The word 'literature' can mean virtually anything that appears in written form. If we want to find out about holidays in Greece, the travel agent will give us some 'literature' about Greece – that is, leaflets and brochures. If we go into a library, we will find books on history, law, philosophy, medicine, and other subjects which are also often called 'literature'. We might hear someone say that they've been looking for information about a particular disease 'in the medical literature'.

But the main use of the word 'literature' is to cover everything where people have used language to create something special as a work of art. We normally divide these works into two main kinds: *fiction* and *non-fiction*. In fiction, people use their imaginations to tell stories, such as the books about Harry Potter, or those by

Roald Dahl or Terry Pratchett. In non-fiction, people talk about the real world, as when they write about their travels or tell the story of someone's life (a *biography*). Sometimes they write stories which are a mix of the two, as when an author writes a tale about Shakespeare which is partly fact and partly fiction.

Most literature in Western society is in written form. We read it. But in many parts of the world, as we saw in Chapter 20, the languages have never been written down. So in these cultures, the people have to listen to literature. They have people who are highly skilled at telling stories and reciting poems. The stories are learned off by heart and told over and over at different times and in different places. This is called 'oral literature'.

Literature in English was like this over a thousand years ago. There's a poem in Old English called *Beowulf*, which is 3,182 lines long. It's a story about a great hero, Beowulf, and his battles with monsters and dragons. The poet would perhaps have recited it, probably accompanying himself on a harp, while everyone was sitting around a fire one evening. It would have taken him about three hours to tell the whole story. Eventually someone wrote it down, which is how we know of it today. It was made into a film in 2007.

Whether oral or written, all literature has one thing in common. The authors are trying to use language in the most effective way. They want the way they speak or write to be beautiful, powerful, dramatic, memorable, original, and to move us in some way. They want to make us feel happy or sad or scared or thrilled or any of a hundred other emotions. They want to make us love some characters and hate others. And they want us to admire the sound and shape of what they've done – in just the same way as we admire a painting, except that authors are painting with words, not colours.

Here's a word picture. It comes from a story written by Charles Dickens called 'A Christmas Carol' about a miser called Scrooge. It's been made into a film several times, including one starring all the Muppets with Michael Caine. This is how Dickens describes Scrooge. Every word is carefully chosen, like adding an extra brush-stroke to a painting.

Oh! but he was a tight-fisted hand at the grindstone. Scrooge! a squeezing, wrenching, grasping, scraping, clutching, covetous old sinner! Hard and sharp as flint, from which no steel had ever struck out generous fire; secret and self-contained, and solitary as an oyster. The cold within him froze his old features, nipped his pointed nose, shrivelled his cheek, stiffened his gait; made his eyes red, his thin lips blue; and spoke out shrewdly in his grating voice. A frosty rime was on his head, and on his eyebrows, and on his wiry chin.

After a description like that, I think we could begin to draw a pretty accurate picture of Scrooge.

Here's another word picture. It's the opening lines of a novel. But this time the author's aim is different. He wants to grip our attention so hard that we just have to read on. This is how he does it, in a single sentence:

It was a warm spring night when a fist knocked at the door so hard that the hinges bent.

We're drawn in straight away. Which door? What fist? It must be a giant at least to bend the hinges. Let's read on:

A man opened it and peered out into the street. There was mist coming off the river and it was a cloudy night. He might as well have tried to see through white velvet.

Now we're getting some mysterious atmosphere. It's foggy. So what sort of thing might knock on the door in the fog ...? We have to read on:

But he thought afterwards that there had been shapes out there, just beyond the light spilling out into the road. A lot of shapes, watching him carefully. He thought maybe there'd been very faint points of light ...

Shapes now. Lots of them. Watching him. More!

> There was no mistaking the shape right in front of him, though. It was big and dark and red and looked like a child's clay model of a man. Its eyes were two embers.

It's very difficult to stop reading at this point and put the book back on the shelf. But I can't carry on because I have to finish my own book. Sorry. (If you haven't read the story, and want to finish it, it's called *Feet of Clay*, and the author is Terry Pratchett.)

Here's one more word picture. A poem this time. William Wordsworth is standing on Westminster Bridge in London on 3 September 1802, and what he sees takes his breath away:

> Earth has not anything to show more fair:
> Dull would he be of soul who could pass by
> A sight so touching in its majesty:
> This City now, doth, like a garment, wear
> The beauty of the morning; silent, bare,
> Ships, towers, domes, theatres, and temples lie
> Open unto the fields and to the sky;
> All bright and glittering in the smokeless air.
> Never did sun more beautifully steep
> In his first splendour, valley, rock, or hill;
> Ne'er saw I, never felt, a calm so deep!
> The river glideth at its own sweet will:
> Dear God! the very houses seem asleep;
> And all that mighty heart is lying still!

Most of us have been in a place where we've looked at a landscape and seen it bright and peaceful like this. We may not have thought about it much at the time. But a poem like this one teaches us how to feel, and how to talk about our feelings. It's so easy to look at things without thinking deeply about them. The job of a poet is to make us *see* and *feel*.

Or sometimes to make us laugh:

Matilda told such Dreadful Lies,
It made one Gasp and Stretch one's Eyes;
Her Aunt, who, from her earliest Youth,
Had kept a Strict Regard for Truth,
Attempted to Believe Matilda:
The effort very nearly killed her ...

That's Hilaire Belloc, in a poem called 'Matilda, Who Told Lies, and was Burned to Death'. Now there's a title to make us read on!

Literature adds a dimension to our lives. Whether we read it as books or on screens, listen to it on audio discs or watch it on DVDs, it captures our hearts and minds in a way that no other artistic method can. We can look at paintings and sculptures, listen to music, and watch dances and ballets, and have some wonderful experiences. But nothing matches the range and depth of detail that comes from using language. Language is the most complex thing human beings ever learn, and it opens up infinite possibilities of self-expression. We'll look more at this claim in Chapter 37.

But before we do, one last word from a poet. A few years ago, Robert Fisher wrote a poem called 'To Find a Poem'. It begins like this:

To find a poem
listen to the wind
whispering words strange and rare
look under stones
there you might find the fossil
shape of an old poem.
They turn up anywhere
in the most unexpected places ...

Even, as you see, in a book about language.

CLERIHEWS

Literature is so diverse. There are all sorts (or 'genres') of novels, plays, and poetry. Sometimes, we can actually pinpoint the birth of a new literary genre.

In the early 1890s, Edward Clerihew Bentley experimented with writing comic poetic biographies of people in four lines. Everybody loved them, and they came to be called 'clerihews'. Here are four of my favourites:

Biography
Is different from Geography.
Geography is about maps,
While Biography deals with chaps.

James Hogg
Kept a dog,
But, being a shepherd
He did not keep a leopard.

Sir Humphry Davy
Was not fond of gravy
He lived in the odium
Of having discovered sodium.

What fools we've been!
We've forgotten the Queen!
She removes her crown, it is said,
When she goes to bed.

Now you've got the idea, try writing one. I don't want to put any ideas into your head, but teachers make quite good subjects …

By the way, Bentley was just 16 when he wrote his first clerihew – the one on Humphry Davy. He thought it up during a science class in his school!

CHAPTER 36

Developing a style

All the authors in Chapter 35 have developed a style of their own. A style is somebody's personal way of using language. It's the same sort of idea as when we're impressed by someone, and we say 'I like your style!' We mean: 'I like the way you do your own thing.' People like to do their own thing with language too.

I should have begun this chapter by saying: all the authors have developed *styles* of their own. Style isn't like our fingerprints. We have different styles, which we develop to suit the different circumstances in which we find ourselves. A better comparison is with the clothes we wear.

If we look inside our wardrobe, what do we see? Most of us have managed to collect quite a range of different kinds of clothes. We have posh clothes for special occasions, casual clothes for everyday, clothes to wear if it's hot, clothes to wear if it's cold, clothes for messing around in, swimming costumes, and lots more. We don't mix them up. We'd be daft if we went out in the snow wearing shorts, or went to the beach on a boiling hot day in a mac. And if we've been invited to a swish party, we dress up for it.

Sometimes we don't have a choice. If we belong to the scouts or guides, or a cadet group, or majorettes, or cheerleaders, or a football team or join the army or the police, then we have to wear a uniform or kit. And sometimes people get an invitation to a reception or a party, and the invitation card tells them what to wear. It might say 'evening dress' or 'lounge suit' or 'fancy dress'. They look inside their wardrobe to see if they've got what they need. If they haven't, either they go out and buy, borrow, or hire something, or they don't go.

As we grow up, we build a language wardrobe inside our heads. Instead of clothes, we have styles. We learn to talk and write in different ways, depending on where we are, who we're talking to, and the impression we want to give of ourselves. We've already seen examples of this in Chapter 11, and again in Chapters 22 and 23. We learn to use formal language for formal occasions and casual language for informal occasions. We learn different kinds of informal language for talking to family, friends, casual acquaintances, and strangers. We learn special ways of talking, such as to animals or little babies, as we saw in Chapter 1. And special ways of writing, as we saw when we looked at text-messaging in Chapter 30.

In school, we learn more formal ways of speaking and writing. We learn new ways of addressing people, by saying 'Sir' or 'Miss'. We find we have to talk and write differently to suit the subject of study. One style of language, we quickly discover, doesn't fit all subjects. The way we lay out the answer to a maths question will be very different from the way we compose an essay in history or geography, write up a science report, or create a piece of imaginative writing. We learn different styles of speaking, too – reading aloud, debating, taking part in a school play.

When we leave school, there are many more styles we have to master. The job we do will make us speak and write in particular ways. I've illustrated several of them already in this book: politicians, advertisers, lawyers, doctors, priests, and so on. But we also have to learn new skills to cope with our life at home. We need to learn how to fill in forms, such as when we apply for a driving licence, a passport, or a place at college or university. When we start getting paid for a job, we have to complete a tax return for the government. And before we get any job at all, we have to write our CV (our 'curriculum vitae' – the record of our achievements and qualifications so far) and send it in.

There are right ways and wrong ways of doing all these things. And if we do things the wrong way, we won't get what we want. If we fill in our passport form wrongly, we won't get a passport. If we send in a CV and don't check our spelling, we probably won't get the job. Filling in a form wrongly might even cost us money. There are some situations where we have to pay a penalty if we get it wrong.

Things are not getting any easier. The number of styles we have to master has virtually doubled, because of the internet. Many of the activities which used to be dealt with through the post are now carried out online. And although there are similarities between filling in a form on paper and filling one in on a screen, there are also lots of differences. These days, everyone has to learn to do things electronically, as well as on paper.

Sometimes, as with clothing, we simply don't have a choice about the kind of language we use. If we are people who go to religious services, the kind of language we use is laid down in advance. People say prayers in a fixed way – often with everyone speaking together. If someone reads aloud from a sacred book, it has to be done in a proper style.

The same principle applies if we find ourselves in court. There, everyone talks in a special way – the judge, the lawyers, the witnesses, the defendants. We might have to take an oath, which means repeating the words exactly as they're said to us. If we give evidence, we have to answer all the questions and do so in a properly respectful way. If we don't, we can be charged with being in 'contempt of court'. And if the judge thinks the offence is serious, we can even be fined or go to prison for it.

So it can pay us to know as much as possible about the different styles that exist in a language, and to master as many of them as we can. And mastering a style means developing a sense of when it's appropriate to use it and when it isn't. If we have a good 'clothes sense', it means we instinctively know what kind of thing to wear to suit the occasion. It's the same with language. We have to develop a good 'language sense' too.

How do we do it? These days schools and colleges often have

courses in 'language skills' or 'language awareness' which give students practice in developing the styles they need. These lay a good foundation for people to build on later in life. In some countries it's possible to follow an examination course which trains and tests students' language awareness, such as the A-level English Language syllabus in the UK. If no such courses exist, it's possible to learn quite a bit about language from other sources, such as online forums – and, of course, by reading books such as this one!

To a large extent, then, style is a matter of conforming to the way people do things. But not everything in style is a matter of being the same as everyone else. There's plenty of scope for being ourselves, such as when we send messages to blogs or forums, write emails and essays, create stories and poems, send texts and tweets, talk to family and friends, make speeches and announcements, think up messages for birthday cards, and do dozens of other everyday activities involving language.

How do we develop our own personal style? One way is to find models that we admire, and copy them. If you think Terry Pratchett is a wonderful writer, try writing like him. If you think Charles Dickens' description of Scrooge is fantastic, try writing your own description of someone in that sort of style. You'll find that some styles come more easily than others. By doing lots of experiments, you'll eventually discover a style that you find comfortable to use. It won't be the same as Pratchett or Dickens, or whoever else you've used as a model. It'll be yours.

Another way is to play about with the rules of your language, to see how they work, and to see if you prefer one way of expressing yourself rather than another. For instance, in a sentence, it's possible to move some words around quite a bit.

> Quickly the soldiers ran across the field.
> The soldiers quickly ran across the field.
> The soldiers ran quickly across the field.
> The soldiers ran across the field quickly.

They all mean the same thing, but the rhythm of each sentence is different, and there are differences of emphasis. If you were writing a story, which would you prefer? The only way to find out is to try out each one, and then choose. But, in order to try out each one, you have to know that there are four options in the first place.

The more you know about the grammar of your language, the more you'll be able to do this kind of thing. Here's an example where there are six options:

Old, ruined, the house scared us all as soon as we saw it.
The old, ruined house scared us all as soon as we saw it.
The house, old, ruined, scared us all as soon as we saw it.
Old and ruined, the house scared us all as soon as we saw it.
The old and ruined house scared us all as soon as we saw it.
The house, old and ruined, scared us all as soon as we saw it.

Which do you like best? There's no 'correct' answer. And you might even find yourself opting for the first one on page 1 of your story and the last one on page 20. When we look carefully at the way professional authors write, we often find variations like that. This is called doing a 'stylistic analysis', and to my mind it's one of the most interesting activities in the study of language.

ARCHY THE COCKROACH'S STYLE

Style is always a matter of choice. A language offers us several ways of saying something, and we choose the one that we think best suits what we want to say or the circumstances in which we say it. For some authors, though, that's not enough. They actually break the normal rules of the language to give themselves a distinctive style. Not using capital letters is a good example.

An American writer called Don Marquis became famous for his stories about a cockroach called Archy and an alley cat called Mehitabel. Archy comes out at night and uses Don Marquis's typewriter to write his poems – but he has a problem. He's too small to press the shift key at the same time as a letter, so he can't make any capitals, and he can't manage punctuation marks. As a result all his poems come out like this one:

if you get gloomy just
take an hour off and sit
and think how
much better this world
is than hell
of course it won t cheer
you up much if
you expect to go there

Not at all bad, for a cockroach!

CHAPTER 37

The complexity of language

Language is the most complex thing human beings ever learn, I said at the end of Chapter 35. Let's reflect for a moment on why that is so.

Look at what you're reading now. Your brain is processing, at great speed, up to 26 letters of the alphabet, some large, some small, and a dozen or so punctuation marks. These letters have been combined into words, and there are (as we saw at the end of Chapter 3) thousands of words to choose from in a language. Many of these words allow different beginnings and endings (such as 'happy', 'unhappy', 'happiness', 'unhappiness'), and there are dozens of these. Then the words are combined into sentences, and there are several thousand ways of doing that. There are thousands more ways of combining the sentences into paragraphs, paragraphs into chapters, and chapters into a whole book. And, along with all this, as we go from one publication to another we have to cope with a huge number of variations in the way language looks on the page – different sizes of type, different typefaces, and so on.

It's the same with speech. If we read out loud, we have to use the sounds of the language – over 40 in the case of English, as we saw in Chapter 5. These are combined into syllables, and there are several hundred ways of doing that – we have to learn that sound-sequences such as 'up', 'shoe', and 'spots' are possible ways of talking in English, but 'ngop', 'shmfi', and 'doprns' aren't. Then, as with writing, we combine these words into sentences. But, unlike writing, we don't talk in paragraphs and chapters. Rather, we talk in conversations and speeches. And, to make these come alive we use hundreds of different tones of voice – the intonation, loudness, speed, and rhythm of our speech.

The purpose of all this? To enable us to say and write whatever we want to. There's no limit. It's amazing, really. Once we've learned a few thousand words, and learned the ways our language allows us to put them together into sentences, we can say things that nobody has ever said before. Here's an example:

> Twelve policemen wearing yellow socks rode donkeys along the beach.

I bet this is the first time anyone has said or written that sentence in the history of the world. I made it up just now, and, even though you've never seen it before, you understood it without any trouble at all. That's what language enables us to do.

In fact, most of the sentences I've written in this book are new. I've never written them before, nor has anyone else. And you've never read them before. Not all the sentences are brand new, of course. I'm not the first person in the universe to have written the sentence I used at the beginning of the previous paragraph, 'The purpose of all this?' I just typed it into Google, and got nearly half a million hits. But I just typed my 'Twelve policemen' sentence into Google, and got no hits. Of course, a search engine doesn't contain everything that's ever been said or written. But it can give us an idea about what's common and what's rare in a language.

We can be even more original, if we want to. If we have a meaning in our head that we want to express, and we can't find the words to say it, then we can make up new words to get our point across. We often create new words by adding 'un-', for instance. Words like these:

> uncool, unchoosy, unfunny, unsorry

Writers have been playing with the language like this for hundreds of years. Over a century ago, Lewis Carroll wrote a scene in *Alice in Wonderland* where Alice meets the Mad Hatter and others sitting round a tea table. It isn't her birthday, so they wish her a merry 'unbirthday'. And about 400 years ago, Shakespeare wrote *Macbeth*, in which he has a character called Malcolm tell several lies about himself. When Malcolm eventually admits that what he was saying wasn't true, he says he will 'unspeak' what he said. Shakespeare loved to invent words like 'unspeak'.

This ability to take familiar bits of language and to combine them to make new words and sentences is what sets language apart from other ways that human beings use to communicate. Look at two people talking to each other. While they're talking, they're also looking at each other, and we can see that the expressions on their faces add a great deal to what they're saying. They smile and frown and look surprised. They might also use their bodies to make gestures, such as by shrugging their shoulders or giving a thumbs-up sign. They might also touch each other, as when they shake hands or kiss. All of these are ways of communicating. But are they 'language'?

No, they're not. People do sometimes use the phrase 'body language' to describe facial expressions, gestures, and touch behaviour. But this isn't 'language' in the sense that we've been using the word in this book. We have to beware the word 'language'. It's often used in a vivid way to mean any kind of connection between people. Here's what someone once wrote in a newspaper review:

The band was brilliant. Every instrument was playing the same language.

What did this mean? It didn't mean that the instruments were speaking English, or French, or whatever. It was a way of describing how well the players worked together. They were showing the same kind of joint understanding as people have when they talk to each other. It's a special use of the word 'language'.

'Body language' shows another special use of the word. When

people use their faces or hands to show their feelings, they're doing something that is very different from what they do when they speak, write, or use a deaf sign language. Here are the main differences:

Differences in scale
How many words are there in a language? Over a million, in the case of a language like English. How many facial expressions are there? Only a few dozen. Maybe a few hundred, if we include all the clever hand movements that appear in some kinds of dancing. But a tiny number, compared with language.

Differences in creativity
We can easily invent new words in a language, as in the case of 'unbirthday'. Can we easily invent new facial expressions? Try it. Invent a new facial expression now. It's not possible. Language is creative in a way that body communication isn't.

Differences in structure
Language has an interesting 'two-level' structure. The actual sounds and letters have no meaning. We can't say that 'p', 'n', or 'i' mean anything. They're just sounds and letters. But as soon as we combine them into words, we have meaning. It's magic: 'pin', 'nip'. Facial expressions aren't like this. They always have a meaning.

We learn many rules of grammar in order to express different meanings, such as changing the order of words in a sentence (as in the 'dog saw the boys' example in Chapter 19). But we don't have rules which change the order of our facial expressions to express different meanings.

I've only talked about facial expressions, in making these points. But the same issues arise when we communicate using gestures or touching.

There's just one situation where gestures become a real language, and that's when deaf people develop them into a sign language, in the way I described in Chapter 18. But deaf signing is totally unlike the casual gestures that hearing people make in their daily lives.

Similarly, our ability to touch can be developed into a real language. This is what happened in the famous case of the twentieth-century writer Helen Keller, who was born deaf and blind. Without the ability to see or hear, she learned to speak by using her hands to feel the movements of the vocal organs of the people around her, and then copying these herself. Again, this sort of thing is totally unlike the casual touching most of us do in everyday life.

Human beings are able to communicate their thoughts and feelings in many different ways. If I have the ability, I can paint them, draw them, sculpt them, dance them, compose them into a symphony or a ballet or a piece of jazz, and express myself in all the ways that are called 'arts and crafts'. Each does something none of the others do. And the word 'language' has been used in relation to all of them. People talk about 'the language of painting', 'the language of music', and so on.

But there's a fundamental difference between all these art forms and 'language' in the sense of this book. When we see a painting or a dance, or listen to a piece of music, we don't need language to enjoy what we see and hear. But if we want to describe what it is that we've seen and heard, or give it a name, or discuss it with others, then we do need language. Language allows us to talk about our experience of the world in a way that no other means of communication can. That's why it is so special. That's why it deserves a book of its own. And that's why it is studied by the subject called *linguistics*.

ANIMALS AND ALIENS

Animals are sometimes said to have language too. People talk about the 'language' of birds, apes, bees, whales, and dolphins, for instance. And it's true that some animal species have developed amazingly sophisticated ways of communicating with each other. When two blackbirds sing to each other, it sounds as if they're having a real conversation.

But there are huge differences between the ways animals communicate and the ways humans do. When animals make a sound, such as a bark or a call, it's an immediate reaction to what's happening around them. If they're scared, they make an alarm call. If they're hungry, they make a hunger call. Animals can't send out a call meaning 'I was scared on Thursday of last week' or 'I'll be hungry later on this afternoon'. Only human language can do things like that.

Zoologists have had some success teaching human language to animals. The most famous experiments have taught chimpanzees to use their hands to make signs to talk about quite a wide range of things. In some cases, the animals have been able to string the signs together to make a simple sentence. It takes a huge amount of training to get them to do this, of course. But it shows that the gap between animal communication and human language may not be as wide as we used to think.

What will be really interesting will be to see if aliens use language in the same way that humans do, or whether they'll talk like R2D2 in *Star Wars*, or use even weirder ways of communicating. Sadly, in most science-fiction films, they all end up speaking English!

CHAPTER 38

Linguistics

Linguistics is the science of language. And the people who study language in this way are called *linguists*. I'm a linguist – and so are you, if you've read this far.

The word 'linguist' has another meaning, of course. It can mean someone who is fluent in several foreign languages – like the amazing Harold Williams mentioned in Chapter 3 who could speak 58 of them. That's a separate skill. I can study music without knowing how to play a lot of musical instruments well. It's the same with linguistics. I can study language without needing to be fluent in lots of languages.

There's a big difference between 'language' and 'languages'. This has been a book about language. It hasn't been an introduction to the different languages of the world. I haven't told you all about French, or German, or Chinese. I might have picked examples from these languages, here and there, but that was always to illustrate a general point. This book has been about the general points. What do all languages have in common? How do they vary? How do people speak, write and sign? How do they learn their language? Why do they use language?

We can study these questions even if we know only one language. People reading this book obviously know English, so most of my examples have been taken from that language. If somebody were to translate this book into another language, they'd need to change the examples too, so that they made better sense to the readers of that language. But they wouldn't need to change the explanations of how language works. The vocal organs I use in order to speak English are exactly the same as those used by a French person in order to speak French – or those used by someone speaking Arabic, Swahili, or Chinese. We all have lungs and tongues and lips. We all have ears and brains. We can study how these organs work regardless of which particular language we happen to speak.

Of course, the more languages we know, the deeper will be our understanding of how language works. It doesn't take long to obtain a basic knowledge of a language. University students of linguistics find they need to spend only a few hours before they're able to grasp the basics of a new language. In as few as 10 hours, working with a speaker of a foreign language, they can find out how to pronounce all the sounds, learn a few hundred words, and master the basic rules of grammar – enough to be able to carry on a simple conversation in that language. They're a long way from being fluent, of course – that would take hundreds of hours, because of all the words that have to be learned. But it's a great start.

The aim of linguistics is not to be fluent in lots of languages. It aims to discover how these languages work. Each of the 6,000 or so languages in the world works in a different way, as we saw in Chapter 19. Each has its own rules of pronunciation, grammar, vocabulary, and conversation. If it's been written down, it has its own rules of spelling and punctuation. Each has its different styles of speaking and writing, its accents and dialects, its literature.

And here's the point: only a few of these languages have been really well studied. Many of the world's languages, indeed, haven't been studied at all. For all we know, they may have some wonderful sounds, words, and sentence patterns that aren't found in any other language. Linguists hunt for these, just as zoologists and botanists do when they go around the world looking for new species of insects or flowers. The trouble is, there are lots of languages and not many linguists. And when we think of all the aspects of language that have to be studied (as outlined in Chapter 37), we can easily see that huge amounts of time are going to be involved.

Even the well-known languages need study. You might think that everything is known about a language like English because people have been investigating it for centuries. Not so. There are hundreds of things still waiting to be discovered. Think of all the accents and dialects, for a start. Many of them have never been described in detail. Or think of the way the language changes. The English we used in the year 2000 is not the same as the English of 2010, and it will change again by 2020. Each year brings new words, new styles, often new pronunciations, spellings, and sentence patterns. And they're all calling out: 'Study me!'

Look at the way the internet is developing. New technology allows us to use language in fresh ways, as we saw in Chapter 29. And many of these fresh ways have been very little studied. Take Twitter, for example, which restricts our messages to 140 characters. What happens to language in such circumstances? Do people abbreviate their words on Twitter, as they do in texting? What sort of sentence patterns do they use? Do they keep their sentences short, or do they use quite long ones? Do boys 'tweet' differently from girls? I don't know the answers to any of these questions – yet.

One of the things linguists do is work out ways of answering these questions. If we wanted to study tweets, how would we set about it? The first thing we'd have to do is make a collection (or 'corpus') of tweets. We'd look carefully through all the examples in our corpus, and see what kind of language turns up. Of course, we have to know about language in order to do that. We have to know about grammar, and vocabulary, and all the other things we've talked about in this book. But, if we've got some of that knowledge inside us, it won't take long before we find ourselves making some interesting discoveries.

All areas of language are like this. Every one of the topics covered in this book opens up a research area. When we look at more advanced books about language, we'll find these areas given their own names. Here are some of them.

- At the end of Chapter 5 I talked about *phonetics*, the

study of speech sounds. A person who studies phonetics is a *phonetician*.

- In Chapter 6, I identified *grammar*, the study of sentence structure. A person who studies grammar is a *grammarian*.
- I've talked a lot about meaning in this book, and especially about vocabulary. All that is part of *semantics*, the study of meaning in language. A person who studies semantics is a *semanticist*.
- I've spent quite a lot of space discussing how language relates to society, through the different accents, dialects, and other varieties we use. All of that is part of *sociolinguistics*. A person who studies sociolinguistics is a *sociolinguist*.
- The study of how children learn language has been an important topic, and that's part of a general study of the relationship between language and the way we think and learn. All of that is studied by *psycholinguistics*. A person who studies psycholinguistics is a *psycholinguist*.
- I've also talked a lot about the way language changes over time, and about the history of sounds, words, and sentences. These topics are studied by *historical linguistics*. People who study historical linguistics are *historical linguists*. They're sometimes called *philologists* too.

This isn't a complete listing of all the branches of linguistics, but I hope it gives you an idea of the many areas of language where people do research, and where exciting discoveries can be made.

There's a bonus, after we study language in this way. We find that our discoveries are not just interesting – they can also be useful. A scientific knowledge of language turns out to be helpful to other people in all kinds of ways. Let's look at some of them.

THE ULTIMATE QUESTIONS

Humans are all born with the same brains and vocal organs, yet by the time they're three years of age they've made great progress in learning to speak one or more of the 6,000 different languages in the world. How do they do it? They wouldn't be able to do it so quickly if their brains weren't 'wired' for language in some way. Are human beings born with a readiness for language built in? A lot of people think so.

They see the baby's brain as having a language mechanism inside it which starts working as soon as someone triggers it. You may remember that I called it a 'language acquisition device' in Chapter 3. It must be a bit like a burglar alarm, which rings automatically as soon as someone sets it off. In the case of language, the trigger is someone speaking to the baby. As soon as the baby hears speech, it starts trying to make sense of it. Is that a sentence? Is that a word? Are those two sounds the same?

If all the languages in the world have certain features in common, maybe these are the features that are built into the human brain. All languages have nouns and verbs, for example. Do babies somehow 'know' about these from the very beginning? And how many other such common features might there be?

For a linguist, there's no topic more important than trying to identify the essential properties of human language. What features define a language? What have all languages got in common? Why are languages different? These are the ultimate questions that linguists one day hope to answer.

CHAPTER 39

Applied linguistics

Language is everywhere. Everybody uses it, and wants to use it well. But quite often people find they can't use it well. And some people find they can't use it at all.

I once knew a little boy called Tom. He was aged four but he was talking like a two-year-old. He was saying such things as 'kick ball' and 'want car', and using lots of one-word sentences, such as those I described in Chapter 4. But he was four, so he should have been saying some really long sentences and telling stories with them. He wasn't. Something had gone terribly wrong.

Quite a few children have what is called a 'language delay'. For some reason they don't learn to speak as quickly as they should. Their friends shoot ahead and they're left behind. As a result, they get very lonely. Nobody wants to talk to you if you can't talk back.

Can anything be done to help these children? Yes. They can go to see a *speech therapist* – a person who's specially trained to work out what's wrong and who knows how to teach language to children. This is what happened to Tom. The speech therapist played some games with him and heard how he talked. She made a recording of his speech, and chatted to his mum and dad about his background. They'd taken Tom to see a doctor, but the doctor hadn't found anything wrong with him. He'd had his hearing checked, and that was fine. He seemed perfectly normal in every way – except he just wasn't talking.

After Tom and his parents had gone home, the therapist listened carefully to the recording she'd made, and worked out exactly what sort of words, sounds, and sentences Tom was using. Then she looked at a chart which showed how language develops in children aged two, three, and four. She could see that Tom was a long way behind.

The next step, she decided, was to teach Tom how to say some new sentences. If he was saying things like 'kick ball', perhaps she could get him to make these sentences a little bit longer. So when Tom came back to see her a few days later, she played language games with him, getting him to say things like 'kick a red ball' and 'kick a blue ball'. Then she got him to say 'The clown is kicking a ball', and other sentences like that. It was a slow process. Tom didn't get the new sentences right straight away. But the therapist was very patient, and after a few more visits he started to make some progress.

Tom went to see his speech therapist twice a week for over a year. During each visit she helped him to use language which was a little bit more difficult than what he had used the week before. The therapy worked. By the time he was five, he had caught up a lot. He wasn't as fluent as other five-year-olds, but he was certainly able to keep his end up in a conversation. And he was able to start school with his friends.

Now let's step back from this story, and think about what skills the speech therapist had to have in order to help Tom.

- She had to know about the way children normally learn to talk, so that she could pinpoint just how far behind other four-year-olds Tom was.
- She had to work out exactly what was wrong with Tom's language, which meant studying his pronunciation, grammar, and vocabulary, and how he got on in a conversation.
- Once she'd done this, she had to think of a path to get Tom from where he was to where he ought to be – from

talking like a two-year-old to talking like a four-year-
old.

- Once she'd started taking him along this path, she had
to keep a careful eye on how he was doing. If she taught
him too slowly, he might get bored. If she taught him too
quickly, he might get confused. The teaching had to be
just right.

- And she also had to give Tom's parents some help and
advice. She was seeing Tom only for half an hour twice
a week. What would happen to him the rest of the time?
The parents would have to do some teaching too. And
she'd have to teach them how to do it.

So it's quite a job, being a speech therapist. They have to know
all about language. And when people are learning to be speech
therapists, they spend a lot of time studying phonetics, grammar,
child language, and many other parts of linguistics. Indeed, language
is such an important subject for them that, in Britain, the name of
their job was changed a few years ago. Speech therapists are now
officially called 'speech and language therapists'. In the USA they're
called 'speech pathologists'.

It's easy to see how the research that linguists do can be helpful
to speech therapists. Linguists helped to draw the road map that the
speech therapist used to guide Tom through the maze of English
sounds, words, and sentences. They carried out many studies of
how normal children learn language. Linguistics is the science of
language, so all the information it uncovers about how language
works and how it is learned and used can be immediately applied
to help solve problems such as Tom's delayed language. And when
linguistics is used to solve problems in this way, it's called *applied
linguistics*.

During the twentieth century, linguists used their special
knowledge to help people improve their services in several fields
where language is a central concern. The field of foreign language
teaching and learning was a particularly important area. Every
day, millions of people do their best to make progress in learning a

foreign language. So questions like these are always being asked:

- How can we find ways to help students learn more easily and efficiently?
- How can we find better methods of language teaching?
- How can we use the latest computer technology to make language learning a more enjoyable process, especially for young people?
- How can we keep teachers and students up-to-date with the way language is changing, so that they learn the latest language and not some out-of-date kind?

These are the sorts of questions which applied linguists explore, when they look inside the language-teaching classroom.

Applied linguists help out in all kinds of situations. Some study the language used in reading schemes in primary schools and suggest new methods for helping young children learn to read. Some work with people whose languages are dying, such as those described in Chapter 20, to see if there are ways of keeping the languages going. Some study the language printed on the things we buy in the shops, to see if it is clear. I once got a doctor's prescription which said 'Take two tablets by mouth every day.' But what did this mean? Did it mean I should take them both together, once a day? Or did it mean I should take one in the morning and one in the evening? It's easy enough to solve the problem, once it's pointed out.

A fascinating area of applied linguistics is in the world of crime detection. We've all seen on TV the arrival of forensic scientists to help solve a crime. They analyse weapons, look for fingerprints, tyre tracks, footprints, and do all sorts of other clever investigations to find out 'who done it'. Forensic linguists do the same sort of thing. They analyse letters, voices, police statements, email records, text messages, chatroom conversations, and all sorts of other pieces of language to find out 'who said it' or 'who wrote it'. If John sends Mary a piece of anonymous hate mail, or forges her signature, it's often possible to prove what's happened from tiny differences in the way the two people use language. If an adult is prowling in a teenage chatroom, and pretending to be 15 years old, a forensic linguist would probably be able to spot him, because his language won't be exactly the same as that used by teenagers.

A rapidly growing area of applied linguistics these days is to help people use the internet better. Sometimes it's quite hard to find our way about. And sometimes we see some very strange things going on. For instance, a few years ago I was reading a Web report about someone who was stabbed to death in an American city street. Then I noticed that there were advertisements down the right side of the screen. The ads said 'Buy your knives here!' and 'Get excellent knives on eBay!'

It's easy to see what the computer had done. It found the word 'knife' in the murder story, and assumed that it meant the kind of knife we use at a dinner table. For this story, the ads down the side of the screen should have been ones to do with safety and crime prevention. What's the solution? Someone needs to analyse the language of the Web page to establish exactly what it is talking about, and then match the page to advertisements that are more suitable. That is what some applied linguists do.

Nobody was doing this kind of research a few years ago. It's one of the new areas of applied linguistics. And that's probably the most exciting thing about the study of language. You never know what's going to happen next. Language moves in totally unexpected directions sometimes. It's never possible to predict the future.

ONE DAY...

It's never possible to predict the future, I said. But we can make some pretty safe guesses. Here are four of them.

We're going to see machines speaking to us more and more. Already, in a car, a satellite navigation system tells us out loud which way to turn. All kinds of other devices will talk to us one day. If I leave a light on in my house, as I go through the front door, some digital device will remind me to go back in and switch it off.

We're going to find ourselves talking to machines more and more. Already there are answerphone systems which will record and playback when we tell them to. And, as I mentioned at the end of Chapter 7, there are washing machines that will boil and spin at our command. To do this, they have to have very good software which will recognize voices, capable of understanding not only our words but also our accent. At present, this software is very limited in what it can do; but one day it will be able to handle everything it hears.

We're going to see machines translating between languages more efficiently. There are already several websites which offer a computer translation service, but the results are often not very good. They'll get a lot better as time goes by.

We're going to be able to see what happens to language in the brain. Already it is possible to use a special scanning machine to see which parts of the brain are most active when we speak, listen, read, and write. One day we'll be able to pinpoint individual sounds, words, and sentence patterns.

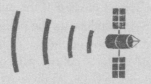

Your language world

I've done my bit. I've told you as much as I can about language, in this little book of 40 chapters. Now it's over to you. People are always telling us that the future of the planet is in our own hands. That's true. And it applies just as much to language as it does to plants, animals, and climate change.

So what should you be concerned about, if you have a real interest in language? I have six big things I care about, and I hope you'll care about them too, and maybe, one day, do something to help make your language world a better place to live in. Because it's your world I'm talking about, not just mine.

I

I hope you'll care about the fact that so many languages in the world are dying. I talked about this in Chapter 20. Half the languages of the world are likely to die out during this century. If their speakers want them saved, are there ways in which you can help? Yes, there are. Saving a language is possible if the public cares enough, and if the politicians care enough. It's the politicians who control the purse-strings that can provide money to help languages survive. And who will vote in those politicians? You will. So: make them realize the importance of language diversity.

II

I hope you'll care about minority languages, even if they're not seriously endangered. Look around you, in whichever country you're reading this, and you'll see dozens of languages being spoken by small groups of people. I talked about this in Chapter 13. These people are as proud of their language as you are of yours. It's part of their identity, and they want it to be treated with respect by others. Their language is as beautiful as ours, and they're proud of it. They'd like to show it off in schools, community centres, libraries, and other areas of public life. Can you help them do this? The first step is to show interest in their languages. If there are other languages spoken in your school, or in your town, make it a priority to find out what they are, and try to get to hear them every now and then.

III

I hope you'll care enough about languages to want to learn as many of them as possible. You don't have to be fluent in them, as I said in Chapter 38. Learn what you need, even if it's only just for listening or reading. Pick up as many bits and pieces of languages as you can – and keep a note of what you've done, using something like the Europass I described at the end of Chapter 13. The important thing is to develop a multilingual personality – to enjoy the variety of languages in the world. Never be scared of trying out a language. Never go to a foreign country without a little dictionary in your pocket. Try using at least one new word every day. And don't worry about making mistakes. I make mistakes all the time, when I try out my languages, and I always get by. Everyone is delighted that I'm having a go.

IV

I hope you'll care about the variety that exists within your own language. That means being interested in all the ways the language varies around the country – the accents and dialects that I talked about in Chapter 12. You don't have to find every accent and dialect equally beautiful, of course, any more than you have to find every style of music equally beautiful. But do try to appreciate the uniqueness of each one, and explore how they came to be the way they are. And don't go round, as many have done in the past, saying that some dialects are 'lazy' or that their speakers sound 'stupid'. An awful lot of people think that you can tell whether people are honest or dishonest just from listening to the way they talk. Do tell them that's rubbish.

V

I hope you'll care about the range of styles that exists within your own language, such as those I talked about in Chapter 35. The danger, especially these days, is that you get so involved in the latest technology, and the opportunities for communication they provide (such as on Facebook or Twitter), that you forget about everything else. Linguists don't go overboard for just one style of language. They try to keep a balance, seeing the way each kind of language does a different job from the others. Keep in mind the comparison with your wardrobe that I made in Chapter 36. You need to be able to handle all kinds of styles, if you want to be at your best in society. And of course that means mastering – really mastering – the standard variety of your language. It means taking as much care as you can to be clear, to avoid ambiguity, and to be in control of all the effects that the language makes available to you. The first step, of course, is to know what these effects are. That's where the study of language comes in.

VI

I hope you'll care about people who are having difficulties learning or using their mother-tongue, and try to help them. I talked about one such little boy in Chapter 39. Those who have problems with speaking have often told me how they've been treated in an unkind way. People seem very ready to poke fun at those who have a lisp, or a stammer, or some other speech difficulty. If you're a real linguist, you won't stand for that sort of thing. And don't be afraid to help people who are having difficulty expressing themselves. For instance, there may be a 'stroke club' in your area, where people meet who've lost their language because a blood vessel has burst in their brain, causing what's called a 'stroke'. They often welcome young people who've got the time to help them talk again. Look around your own school. People who have a speech problem are often lonely, because they can't talk to others in a normal way. You might be able to help there too.

Language is different from every other subject you'll ever study, because language is a part of everything you'll ever study. It's there outside school too, forming a part of everything you do. Even if you have an experience which doesn't involve language – such as listening to music at a concert or looking at a painting – you'll want to talk about it afterwards.

Language never leaves you alone. It's there in your head, helping you to think. It's there to help you to make relationships – and to break them. It's there to remind you who you are and where you come from. It's there to cheer you up – and to cheer others up, if they're feeling low.

Language doesn't do everything. Sometimes there are no words for what we want to say. Sometimes it's better just to give someone a hug. People sometimes say: 'A picture is worth a thousand words.' That's true. But language is never far away. To talk about the picture, you may need a thousand words.

We have to learn when to use language and when not to. Here's another saying: 'speech is silver, silence is golden.' The proverb is reminding us that we shouldn't blather on too much. We need to shut up every now and again. That's good advice. But what do we do in the silence? We listen to what others are saying. And listening is part of language too.

This is a 'little book' about language. But language is a big subject. None bigger, to my mind. It's the Mount Everest of subjects. I suppose that's why I find it all so fascinating. And if you've stayed with me all the way to this final page, I hope you now do too.

Index